The Celtic Way of Evangelism

THE CELTIC WAY OF EVANGELISM

HOW CHRISTIANITY CAN REACH THE WEST...AGAIN

TENTH ANNIVERSARY REVISED AND EXPANDED EDITION

GEORGE G. HUNTER III

ABINGDON PRESS
Nashville

THE CELTIC WAY OF EVANGELISM
HOW CHRISTIANITY CAN REACH THE WEST . . . AGAIN

Library of Congress Cataloging-in-Publication Data
Hunter, George G., 1938-
 The Celtic way of evangelism : how Christianity can reach the West— again / George G. Hunter III. — 10th anniversary rev. and expanded ed.
   p. cm.
 Includes bibliographical references (p.   ) and index.
 ISBN 978-1-4267-1137-4 (book - pbk./trade pbk., adhesive - perfect binding : alk. paper) 1. Celtic Church. 2. Evangelistic work—Western countries. I. Title.
 BR748.H86 2010
 266.0089'916—dc22

                                                                                    2010035192

All scripture quotations are taken from the New Revised Standard Version of the Bible, copyright 1989, Division of Christian Education of the National Council of the Churches of Christ in the United States of America. Used by permission. All rights reserved.

The poem on pages 67-68 is taken from *The Celtic Churches: A History* A.D. *200 to 1200* by John T. McNeill, copyright © 1974 by The University of Chicago Press. All rights reserved. Used by permission of The University of Chicago Press.

Selections from *How the Irish Saved Civilization: The Untold Story of Ireland's Historic Role from the Fall of Rome to the Rise of Medieval Europe* by Thomas Cahill are copyright © 1995 by Thomas Cahill. Used by permission of Doubleday, a division of Random House, Inc.

The poem on pages 23-24, "Exams," is from *Celtic Prayers for Everyday Life: Prayers for Every Occasion* by Ray Simpson. Copyright © 1998 by Ray Simpson. All rights reserved. Reproduced by permission of Hodder & Stoughton Limited.

We acknowledge the Four Courts Press, Dublin, Ireland, for kind permission to quote from *St. Patrick's World* by Liam de Paor.

10 11 12 13 14 15 16 17 18 19—10 9 8 7 6 5 4 3 2 1

MANUFACTURED IN THE UNITED STATES OF AMERICA

With gratitude for
Orville Nelson, Henry Barnett, Charles T. Thrift,
William R. Cannon, Mack Stokes, Claude Thompson,
Norman Perrin, Ted Runyon, Bill Mallard,
Donald Soper, Bryan Green, Donald McGavran,
Lawrence Lacour, Kermit Long, Ira Galloway,
Leroy Howe, Harold Bales, Rueben Job,
Ed Beck, John Ed Mathison, Ken Kinghorn,
John Jellicorse, Edward T. Hall, Joe Quillian,
Stephen Neill, E. Stanley Jones, Alan Walker,
and other professors, mentors, role models, heroes, and colleagues
who inspired me to learn beyond what anyone taught me
and to invest a lifetime in rethinking Christianity's effective mission

CONTENTS

PREFACE TO THE SECOND EDITION

hen the first edition of this book was published as the third millennium began, the Western world faced populations that were increasingly secular—people with no serious Christian background or memory, unfamiliar with what Christians believe, experience, and live for. These populations were increasingly urban; as they left their traditional communities and became immersed in the city's crowding, competitiveness, and consumerism, they often felt disillusionment or alienation; and removed from nature, they were out of touch with God's natural revelation.

These populations were also increasingly postmodern. They had given up on the Enlightenment's ideology and promises; they became more peer driven, feeling driven, and right-brained than their forebears. Furthermore, these populations were increasingly neobarbarian; they lacked the etiquette, the refinement, the class, and other traits of "civilized people," and their lives were often out of control. These populations were also increasingly receptive—exploring worldview options from astrology to Zen. They were looking for life, but "in all the wrong places."

With the publication of the tenth anniversary revised edition of *The Celtic Way of Evangelism*, the West's mission fields today are much like they were a decade ago, but more so. More people are more secular, urban, postmodern, and neobarbarian today. Recent history has added at least two features. In the last decade, evangelical

Christianity has lost some public credibility, and atheism has now become almost as chic in Great Britain and the United States as in continental Europe.

In the face of this changing post-Christian Western culture, more church leaders than before are now clear that our churches are placed in mission fields, and more churches have moved to a more apostolic or missional understanding of their main business. I am told that this book's first edition contributed to that paradigm shift. The majority of Western church leaders, however, are still in denial; they still plan and do church as though next year will be 1957.

Furthermore, most of the Western church leaders who are not in denial do not know *how* to engage the epidemic numbers of secular, postmodern, neobarbarians outside (or even those inside) their churches. Moreover, most of the minority of church leaders who *do* know what to do are intuitively gifted people who cannot teach others much of what they know, and some are charismatic leaders who cannot (yet?) be cloned. Most church leaders in the West still feel that they lack both the precedent and the paradigm for engaging the West's emerging mission fields. So I continue to commend and interpret an ancient model from which Western Christians can draw as they face this daunting challenge. This ancient movement, now known as "Celtic Christianity," calls to us from the second half of the first millennium and shows us the way forward in the third millennium.

Although some Western church leaders have been impressed by the late Robert Webber's "ancient-future" perspective, the idea has still not registered with most leaders. The idea that ancient Celtic Christianity could reveal our way forward is not one of their conscious options for at least two reasons. First, they assume that *no* early medieval expression of Christianity could possibly be relevant to the challenges we now face. Second, they assume that the only useful stream of insight is, by definition, confined to Roman Christianity and its Reformation offshoots. Few of us study other churches and Christian movements of the past or the present.

The typical church history course virtually ignores most of Christianity's experience from most periods of history. The assumption is blatant: the only church history really worth knowing is Latin church history and its Reformation spin-offs. When a colleague heard I was writing the first edition on how the ancient Celtic Christians did ministry and mission, he asked, "What could we possibly learn from them?"

In the 1990s, when I led field seminars on Celtic evangelism, a few people who were already "into" Celtic music, art, poetry, dance, or spirituality brought interest to the subject, as well as those who were interested in recovering their Irish or Scottish roots. Most people, however, brought low expectations, wondering why Hunter would risk boring people with his new antiquarian obsession! The openness to these ideas is much greater today.

Two books were published in the 1990s that put the topic on more people's "maps" and stimulated wider interest in Celtic Christianity. Thomas Cahill's *How the Irish Saved Civilization* told the story, with great flair, of the Celtic movement's evangelization of Ireland, Scotland, England, and western Europe. John Finney's *Recovering the Past* sketched the basic way that the Celtic Christian movement approached mission as compared to the establishment Roman way. This project stands on the shoulders of Cahill and Finney.

Two other sources were immensely useful. Liam de Paor's *Saint Patrick's World* collected, in English translation, the ancient Gaelic and Latin sources that tell us much of what is knowable about Saint Patrick, his mission, and his movement's history in the centuries that followed. The Oxford University Press edition of Bede's *Ecclesiastical*

History of the English People, with many endnotes, makes this classic history of the post-Irish expansion of Celtic Christianity even more useful than before. (Another marvelous collection of sources, *Celtic Spirituality*, edited by Oliver Davies, was published too late to inform my first edition. Alas, I discovered Máire B. de Paor's marvelous commentary on Patrick's *Confession*, *Patrick: The Pilgrim Apostle of Ireland*, too late for the first edition.)

De Paor and Bede were indispensable because I approached this topic as a communication theorist and missiologist, with no card-carrying credentials as a historian and glaring deficiencies for interpreting ancient and medieval history. My Latin and Greek are beyond rusty. I have no knowledge of Irish Gaelic, any other Celtic language, or any of the languages employed as Celtic Christians reached the "barbarian" peoples of Europe. At least one source by a "real historian," *The Quest for Celtic Christianity* by Donald E. Meek, argues (repeatedly) that people who are not competent in *all* of the source languages have *no* business writing about the movement. (Since I could find *no* significant insights relevant to this project in his *Quest* that were not available from English-translation sources, and since the writer was oblivious to many questions that mission scholars know to ask of historical data, I rediscovered that the history of the Christian movement is too important to leave entirely to the desk historians!)

Some critics may charge that I have reached some conclusions on insufficient evidence. That charge may, indeed, be valid; some of my conclusions are based on less data than good scholarship prefers, for two reasons. (1) We do not have as much data from the ancient movement as we would like, and some of what we have can be interpreted in two (or more) ways. (2) If, from multiple disciplines, however, we know that all (or most) effective Christian advocates do certain things, that all (or most) Christian movements do certain things, that all (or most) primal peoples respond to the gospel in certain ways, or that all (or most) pre-Christian people experience Christian conversion in certain ways, then we can reasonably risk similar conclusions about Celtic Christianity with less evidence than if Celtic Christian sources were our only sources.

This second edition has been substantially revised. There are changes on every page and in most paragraphs. Some paragraphs have been deleted; others added. The book is now also expanded. The fifth chapter interprets the movement's achievement in communicating the gospel from additional insights in communication theory. This edition adds a new next-to-last chapter that addresses the interest of twenty-first-century Western church leaders in the formation of Christians, from a Celtic perspective. The last chapter is updated and adds a cogent summary of some of the book's key insights.

Some readers may want to know that several of my other books develop some of this book's themes in greater range or depth. See, especially, *How to Reach Secular People* (Abingdon Press, 1992), *Radical Outreach: The Recovery of Apostolic Ministry and Evangelism* (Abingdon Press, 2003), and *The Apostolic Congregation: Church Growth Reconceived for a New Generation* (Abingdon Press, 2009).

I continue to thank the institutions, lectureships, seminars, and symposia, now too numerous to mention, that invited me to present these ideas, whose people provided invaluable feedback. I continue to reflect upon the days spent in "solitary" at the site of Patrick's first church (Saul), at his grave (in Downpatrick), and at the ancient sites of Glendalough, Iona, and Lindisfarne, where my soul experienced some of the vision that once drove apostolic teams of men and women to abandon almost everything they cherished for the sake of lost populations who needed to be found.

The first edition was presented with the naive confidence that, if Western church leaders were willing to love the Lord of the Harvest with their minds as well as their hearts, and were willing to learn from a once-great movement outside of the Roman paradigm, then Christianity could become contagious once more across North America and Europe. In the past decade, I discovered that the project's driving ideas were even more relevant for navigating a secular postmodern mission field than I had perceived. So I present this second edition with the confidence that our appropriation of Celtic Christianity's vision and approach will gain momentum in the decade ahead.

CHAPTER 1

The Gospel to the Irish

round A.D. 400, Patricius (Patrick) was growing up in what is now northeast England. His people were "Britons," one of the "Celtic" peoples then populating the British Isles, though Patrick's aristocratic family had gone "Roman" during the Roman occupation of England. So Patrick, culturally, was as much Roman as Celtic; his first language was Latin, though he understood some of the "Welsh" spoken by the lower classes. His family was Christian; his grandfather was a priest. Patrick was baptized, he had acquired some Christian teaching, and he knew the catechism, but he became only a very nominal Christian; he enjoyed ridiculing the clergy, and in the company of other "ungoverned" youth, he lived toward the wild side.[1]

When Patrick was sixteen, a band of Celtic pirates from Ireland invaded his homeland. They captured Patrick and many other young men, forced them onto a ship, sailed to Ireland, and sold them into slavery. The pirates sold Patrick to a prosperous tribal chief and Druid named Miliuc (Miliuc moccu Boin), who put Patrick to work herding cattle. Patrick lived the next six years in two settings. He spent blocks of time in Miliuc's settlement with the people, and he probably resided in a compound with other Briton slaves—some of whom were Christians, who would have welcomed Patrick into their fellowship. He spent other blocks of time in wilderness areas managing a herd of cattle, perhaps assisted by an industrious border collie or Welsh corgi.

During his six years of enslavement in these two settings, Patrick experienced three profound changes. First, in the periods when Patrick was herding cattle in a wilderness area, he experienced what theologians call God's "natural revelation." He sensed, with the seasons, the creatures, the nights under the stars, and the ever-present winds, the presence of God; he identified this presence with the triune God he had learned about in the catechism and had heard about from his people back home and from his Christian peers in Miliuc's compound. In his (more or less) autobiographical *Confession* Patrick tells us,

> After I had arrived in Ireland, I found myself pasturing flocks daily, and I prayed a number of times each day. More and more the love and fear of God came to me, and faith grew and my spirit was exercised, until I was praying up to a hundred times every day and in the night nearly as often.[2]

Patrick became a devout Christian, and the profound change was obvious to his captors.

Second, Patrick changed in another way during the periods he spent with his captors in their settlement. He came to understand the Irish Celtic people, and their language and culture, with the kind of intuitive insight that is usually possible only, as in Patrick's case, from the underside. Miliuc's people knew that this slave understood them.

Third, in time Patrick came to love his captors, to identify with them, and to hope for their reconciliation to God. One day, he would feel that they were his people as much as the Britons were.

One night, after six years of captivity, a voice spoke to Patrick in a dream, announcing the good news of his imminent freedom. The voice instructed him to awaken early and walk to a seacoast: "Your ship is ready!" He walked for several days, reached the seacoast, saw the promised ship, and negotiated his way on board.

The data for piecing together the next quarter century of Patrick's story are limited, and scholars fuss over the scant data we have, but the story line runs something like this. The ship probably took Patrick to Gaul, though perhaps to England or Rome. He spent time in Gaul (with the monastic community of Saint Martin of Tours), and he probably spent time in Rome, but mainly he returned to his people in England. He trained for the priesthood—perhaps in Rome or in Gaul, more likely in England. His training immersed his mind in the Scriptures and grounded him in the basic orthodox theology that prevailed in the Western church of the time before Saint Augustine's mighty influence. He then served for years as a faithful parish priest in England.

One night years later Patrick experienced another dream that was to change his life again. An angel named Victor approached him with letters from his former captors in Ireland. As he read one of the letters, he "imagined in that moment that [he] heard the voice of those very people who were near the wood of Foclut, . . . and they cried out, as with one voice 'We appeal to you, holy servant boy, to come and walk among us.'"[3]

When Patrick awakened the next morning, he interpreted the dream as his "Macedonian call" to take Christianity's gospel to the Celtic peoples of Ireland. He proposed to his ecclesiastical superiors that he be sent on this mission. The bishops of the British church, probably with the strong encouragement of Pope Celestine, affirmed Patrick's vision. Patrick was ordained a bishop and appointed to Ireland as history's first missionary bishop. The tradition tells us that he arrived in Ireland with an "apostolic team" of priests, seminarians, and laymen and laywomen in (or about) A.D. 432.[4]

Patrick's mission to Ireland was to be such an unprecedented undertaking that it is impossible to overstate its significance or the magnitude of the challenge they faced. Why? Because the Irish Celtic peoples were "barbarians."

Perhaps the oldest and most perennial issue in the history of Christianity's world mission hangs upon two terms: *Christianizing* and *civilizing*. In a classic essay, Pierce Beaver tells us that mission leaders, including the Protestant mission leaders of the last several hundred years, have usually assumed that the two goals of a Christian mission are to "evangelize" a people and to "civilize" them. Beaver explains that, in the formative period of Protestant mission, there was never even

> debate about the legitimacy of the stress on the civilizing function of missions. Debate was only about priority; which came first, christianization or civilization? Some held that a certain degree of civilization was first necessary to enable a people to understand and accept the faith. Others argued that one should begin with christianization since the gospel inevitably produced a hunger for civilization. Most persons believed that the two mutually interacted and should be stressed equally and simultaneously.[5]

In practice, a Protestant mission's civilizing objectives for a people were scripted more by the culture of the sending nation than by Scripture. Beaver reports, for instance, that in the sixteenth- to eighteenth-century period of Spain's colonial expansion, "Spain . . . endeavored to transplant Christianity and civilization both according to the Spanish model."[6] Likewise, the seventeenth-century Puritan mission to Native Americans organized converts into churches and into "Christian towns" in order to enculturate the Indians into what Cotton Mather called "a more decent and English way of living."[7] Beaver reports that "even in countries with a high culture, such as India and China,

European missionaries stressed the 'civilizing' objective as much as their brethren in primitive regions because they regarded the local culture as degenerate and superstitious—a barrier to christianization."[8]

The much earlier period of Roman Christianity's expansion, prior to Patrick, had struggled with these same issues but was afflicted by two versions of this problem, both different from the later Protestant versions. The perspective of the ancient Roman Christian leaders can be baldly stated in two points: (1) Roman Christian leaders assumed that some civilizing had to come *first*. A population had to already be civilized "enough" to become Christianized; some degree of civilization was a prerequisite to Christianization. (2) Then, once a sufficiently civilized population became Christian, they were expected in time to read and speak Latin, to adopt other Roman customs, to do church the Roman way, and in other ways to become culturally Roman people.

This Roman perspective seems to have surfaced in the second century and then prevailed until the time of Patrick. The first-century apostolic movement reached several peoples, at least, who were neither civilized nor subsequently Romanized. The apostolic tradition reports, for instance, that Andrew planted Christianity among barbarian populations of Scythia, that Thomas reached Parthians and Syrians, and that Matthew's martyrdom ignited a Christian movement in a cannibal population named the Anthropophagi.[9]

From the second century on, however, historians report no organized missions to the "barbarian" peoples, such as the Celts, the Goths, the Visigoths, the Vandals, the Franks, the Frisians, the Huns, and the Vikings, who lived at the fringes of the Roman Empire.[10] By now, the Church assumed that reaching barbarians was impossible; a population, by definition, had to be literate and rational enough to understand Christianity, and cultured and civil enough to become "real" Christians if they did understand it.

Why did the Roman Church regard the Irish Celts as barbarians? What could have given them that idea? The Romans did not know the Irish people. Ireland was geographically isolated from the Roman Empire; Rome had never conquered or controlled Ireland, or even placed a Roman colony there.

Historically, however, Romans had observed other Celtic peoples, and they had heard about the Irish. The history of the Keltoi peoples predated the Roman Empire by more than a thousand years. Celtic tribes had once been the dominant population of Europe, and they had been the greatest warriors of Europe. The European Celts were not a race, with a common genetic lineage, so much as a macroculture—a linguistic and cultural family of peoples. However, each Celtic tribe was distinct from the others, with its own gods, laws, customs, and language or dialect.[11]

Consequently, the Celtic tribes had little experience in organizing across tribal lines. So, in warfare, each Celtic tribe fought for itself but was not organized to fight in league with other tribes against a common enemy. An analogy should clarify this important point. A zoologist once informed me that a tiger will defeat a lion in battle, but five lions will defeat five tigers because the lions fight as a team and the tigers do not. The five lions take on one tiger at a time. Each Celtic tribe was a formidable tiger in battle, greatly respected and feared. The Romans, with legendary strength in organization and coordination, were the lions in a lengthy series of battles against specific tribes to incrementally expand their empire.

For two centuries, the lions pushed the tigers westward to the Celtic fringe of western Europe—places like Gaul, Brittany, and the British Isles. In Patrick's time, the British Isles featured several Celtic peoples—most notably the Britons in what is now England, the Picts in what is now Scotland, and the Irish (or the Scots) in Ireland. In the two centuries following Patrick, hordes of the Irish invaded

Scotland and absorbed the Picts, thus accounting for the term *Scots-Irish* and explaining the similarities in Scottish and Irish accents and culture to this day.

So the Romans had observed some Celtic peoples historically; indeed, Julius Caesar had even written about them. Furthermore, the Romans had heard many rumors about the Irish Celts. Why did the Romans think of the Celtic peoples, particularly the Irish, as barbarians? They reached this conclusion for at least five reasons: (1) The Romans tended to regard everyone who wasn't culturally Roman as barbarian.[12] (2) The Romans regarded literacy as a sure and certain sign of being civilized; the Irish Celts, with a rich oral tradition, did not read and write and were not interested in doing either one. (3) The Irish were known to be "emotional" people, volatile personalities who expressed the full range of human emotions, which could get out of control. The Romans believed that emotional control was essential to being civilized. (4) In warfare "all the Celts . . . stripped before battle and rushed their enemy naked, carrying sword and shield but wearing only sandals and torc—a twisted, golden neck ornament . . . [while] howling and, it seemed, possessed by demons!"[13] (Roman soldiers would have noticed that!) (5) Furthermore, the Celts were known to decapitate some conquered enemy warriors[14] and to practice human sacrifice in some of their religious rituals.[15] For such reasons, the Romans stereotyped the Irish Celts as barbarians, and therefore probably unreachable.[16] Nevertheless, by Patrick's time there was some interest, especially at the papal level, in the possibility of reaching barbarians, and that is probably why Patrick's Macedonian vision found Pope Celestine's support.

Patrick's mission to Ireland was unprecedented and was widely assumed to be impossible. The Irish context of that period, however, provided strategic advantages for Patrick's mission. Ireland was populated by about 150 tuaths—extended tribes—each tribe fiercely loyal to its tribal king.[17] Ireland's total population numbered between 200,000 and 500,000 people.[18] By Patrick's time, all of the tribes spoke the same language that Patrick had learned while a slave, and they now shared more or less the same culture, so Patrick understood them.

Indeed, the fact that Patrick understood the people and their language, their issues, and their ways serves as the most strategically significant insight that was to drive the wider expansion of Celtic Christianity and stands as perhaps our greatest single learning from this movement. There is no shortcut to understanding the people. When you understand the people, you often know what to say and do and how. When the people know that the Christians understand them, they infer that maybe Christianity's High God understands them too.

Brendan Lehane identifies other contextual factors conducive to a Christian movement in fifth-century Ireland.[19] For perhaps one thousand years, no outside religion had penetrated Ireland, so without a tradition of suspicion, the Irish gave Christian advocates a willing hearing. Philosophically, the Irish were accustomed to paradox, which prepared them to appreciate some of Christianity's central truth claims. Their belief that Ultimate Reality is complex, and their fascination with rhetorical triads and the number three opened them to Christianity's triune God. Christianity's contrasting features of idealism and practicality engaged identical traits in the Irish character. No other religion could have engaged the Irish people's love for heroism, stories, and legends like Christianity. Some of Christianity's values and virtues essentially matched, or fulfilled, ideals in Irish piety and folklore. Irish Christianity was able to deeply affirm and fulfill the Irish love for nature and nature's creatures, and the Irish belief in the closeness of the Divine. Christianity fueled and amplified the Irish love for learning and adapted to the

Irish preference for oral tradition and memorizing rather than writing and reading. Christianity's strategic approach contrasted, however, with what the Irish had observed in their primal religion. The Druids, Ireland's traditional religious leaders for centuries, had enhanced their status and power through closely guarding their secret knowledge. The people easily perceived the difference in Christianity, which was "open to all, it kept no secrets from anyone, and had as its aim the happiness of the whole population."[20]

After years of reflection on how the Irish might be reached, Patrick moved into mission. We do not know nearly all we would like to know about his movement's approach and methods, though our discussion of the Irish context included several answers. Often, his writings tantalize us more than they inform us. Moreover, we cannot be certain how much of the Celtic Christian movement's later approach in Ireland, Scotland, England, and Europe was pioneered and modeled by Patrick and how much his successors developed the approach after him. But from a handful of ancient sources,[21] we can piece together the following outline of a typical approach, which undoubtedly varied from one time and setting to another.

Patrick's apostolic band would have included a dozen or so people, including priests, seminarians, laymen, and laywomen.[22] Upon arrival at a tribal settlement, Patrick would engage the king and other opinion leaders, hoping for their conversion[23] or at least their clearance to camp near the people and form into a community of faith adjacent to the tribal settlement. The apostolic (in the sense of the Greek word meaning "sent on mission") team would meet the people, engage them in conversation and in ministry, and look for people who appeared receptive. They would pray for sick people and for possessed people, and they would counsel people and mediate conflicts. On at least one occasion, Patrick blessed a river and prayed for the people to catch more fish. They would engage in some open-air speaking, probably employing parable, story, poetry, song, visual symbols, visual arts, and perhaps drama to engage the Celtic people's remarkable imaginations. Often, we think, Patrick would receive the people's questions and then speak to those questions collectively.[24]

The apostolic band would probably welcome responsive people into their group fellowship to worship with them, pray with them, minister to them, converse with them, and break bread together.[25] One band member or another would probably join with each responsive person to reach out to relatives and friends. The mission team typically spent weeks or months as a ministering community of faith within the tribe. The church that emerged within the tribe would have been astonishingly indigenous.

If God blessed the efforts of Patrick's band and the people responded in faith, they built a church. Indeed, the salient goal of the mission to each settlement was to plant a church, and Patrick often led in the decision regarding the chapel's location. Sometimes one to several members of the team would fan out and reach a nearby community. On one occasion, a young nun named Mathona "went across the Mountain . . . and founded a free church at Tamnach."[26] Chapels were small so, from the beginning, the church in most settlements would have served multiple congregations. The founding of a church would have involved a public service in which the church's first converts were baptized into the faith. When the apostolic team moved on, Patrick would leave one of his protégés behind to be the new church's priest, "leaving with [him] a textbook of elementary Christian instruction."[27] Typically, one or two of the settlement's young people, who would one day be priests or nuns, would join the team as it moved on to another tribal settlement to plant another church.[28] Patrick engaged in this group approach to apostolic ministry until his death around A.D. 460. As the movement grew, he devoted more of his time to administration, preparing and ordaining priests, and, like Paul before him, visiting the churches he had planted. By this time, however, other leaders were leading apostolic bands in more and more missions to Irish settlements.

What had Patrick and his people achieved in his twenty-eight-year mission to the barbarian Irish Celts? The question cannot be answered with mathematical precision, but estimates are possible. We believe there were some Christians, perhaps expatriate Christian slaves or traders and their families, already living in Ireland by A.D. 432, but there was no indigenous Christian movement to the Irish before Patrick. Patrick and his people launched a movement. They baptized "many thousands" of people, probably tens of thousands. Tirechan refers, usually by name, to at least fifty-five churches that Patrick's team planted, essentially in the one province of Connacht. The tradition has Patrick engaging in substantial ministry in northern, central, and eastern Ireland, with some forays beyond. An ancient document called the "Annals of the Four Masters" reports that Patrick's mission planted about seven hundred churches and that Patrick ordained perhaps one thousand priests.[29] Within his lifetime, 30 to 40 (or more) of Ireland's 150 tribes became substantially Christian. Louis Gougaud offers this assessment:

> Most certainly he did not succeed in converting all the heathens of the island; but he won so many of them for Christ, he founded so many churches, ordained so many clerics, kindled such a zeal in men's hearts, that it seems right to believe that to him was directly due the wonderful outblossoming of Christianity which distinguished Ireland in the following ages.[30]

Patrick's apostolic achievement included social dimensions. To our knowledge, he was the first public European leader to speak and crusade against slavery. Within his lifetime, or soon after, "the Irish slave trade came to a halt, and other forms of violence, such as murder and intertribal warfare, decreased," and his communities modeled the Christian way of faithfulness, generosity, and peace to all the Irish.[31]

One would naturally assume that the British church, which had ordained Patrick a bishop and sent him to Ireland, would have continued to affirm his mission and celebrate its achievements. This was far from the case. The generation of British bishops, who succeeded the bishops who originally sent Patrick, did not "own" their predecessors' priorities. Some of them, perhaps most, criticized him savagely. This criticism stung Patrick and aroused him to write the *Confession* that explained and defended his mission.

What was the "beef" of the British church leaders? They seem to have defined two roles (only) for a bishop: administrator and chaplain. Therefore, a bishop's primary (perhaps only) expectations were to administer the existing churches and care for faithful Christians. (A local priest's job description was similar, stressing pastoral care of the local flock.) So the British leaders were offended and angered that Patrick was spending priority time not with church people but with pagans, sinners, and barbarians.

This perspective surfaced in the earliest phase of the Christian movement. First-century Pharisees and Sadducees savagely criticized Jesus of Nazareth for practicing the same kind of scandalous fraternizing priorities that Patrick now practiced. (Such population groups as people who were blind, deaf, mentally disabled or possessed; prostitutes and Samaritans; tax collectors and Zealots—whom Jesus publicly engaged and befriended—were not even permitted inside the Temple. So his ministry to such people, and his teaching that the kingdom of God was for them also, scandalized the religious establishment.) Furthermore, this perspective is astonishingly widespread today.

Pastors and churches today who regard outreach to lost people as the church's main business, and especially those who are perceived to prefer the company of lost people to the company of church people, are suspect, marginalized, and "shot at" by establishment Christians and church leaders. No major denomination in the United States regards apostolic ministry to card-carrying, secular, pre-Christian outsiders as its priority or even as normal ministry.

Patrick seized the high ground. Implicitly, he reminded his detractors of what it means to serve in apostolic succession—that is, to succeed the ancient apostles in their mission to pre-Christian populations. Explicitly, he defended his calling in terms of the biblical mandate to evangelize the world's peoples. Patrick explained that he devoted his life to helping Irish populations be "reborn in God" and "redeemed from the ends of the earth," because the Church is placed in the world "as a light among the nations"; so our calling is to "fish well" and "to spread our nets so that we can catch a great . . . multitude for God." The Church, he reminded them, is commanded by the risen Christ to go into "all the world," "to preach the gospel to all creation," and to "teach all nations" in anticipation of "the last days" when the Lord "will pour out [his] spirit over all flesh" and make peoples who were not his into "children of the living God." So, Patrick wrote, "this is why it came about in Ireland that people who had no acquaintance with God . . . are recently . . . made a people of the Lord and are known as children of God. . . . For God gave me such grace, that many people through me were reborn to God and afterward confirmed and brought to perfection."[32]

Chapter 2

A New Kind of Community, a New Kind of Life

 rish Christianity spread even more in the generations following the death of Patrick than it had in Patrick's lifetime. Since we have no written records from that period, our knowledge of how the Irish church grew in its first century is spotty, but two facts are paramount. First, the available evidence suggests that, in measurable time, the movement blanketed the island: "In Ireland alone, there are more than 6,000 place names containing the element Cill—the old Gaelic word for church."[1] Second, Irish Christianity was geographically beyond the reach of Rome's ability to shape and control, so a distinctively Celtic approach to doing church and living out the Christian life and witness emerged.

What would a visitor from Rome have noticed about Celtic Christianity that was different? The visitor would have observed more of a movement than an institution, with small provisional buildings of wood and mud; a movement featuring laity more than clergy in ministry. This movement, compared to the Roman wing of the One Church, was more imaginative and less cerebral, closer to nature and its creatures, and emphasized the immanence and providence of the triune God more than his transcendence.

Most of all, the Roman visitor would notice that Patrick's "remarkable achievement was to found a new kind of church, one which broke the Roman imperial mould and was both catholic and barbarian."[2] That "new kind of church" essentially added, to the settlement or parish church, a second dominant form of Christian community; and influences from this second form reshaped the first. I call this second form the "monastic community." Patrick's leadership had indigenized Christianity to Irish cultural soil more than anyone else was attempting anywhere else. Since Patrick refers to "monks" and "virgins for Christ" in his writings, we can presume that he and his people started monastic communities in his lifetime. These communities proliferated in the generation following Patrick's death. Some writers believe he started monastic communities somewhat like he had observed at Saint Martin's community in Gaul.[3] It is more likely that he learned from Martin's model and from the monasticism of the Eastern church, but adapted from both models.

The movement also planted many churches in Irish settlements, each with a priest, with a group of churches administered by a bishop, and which, in other ways, somewhat resembled the established Roman way of doing church. However, the parish church model did not really fit ancient Irish life. The Roman model presupposed an organized town or village, with a parish church at the town's center. It also presupposed a network of towns, connected by roads, within a geographic political unit (like a county) that could double as a bishop's diocese. Celtic Ireland probably had no established towns, however, only provisional settlements of tribal groups; the group might move on to better grazing. Ireland had no official political units or boundaries. Furthermore, Ireland had few, if any, roads more useful than a Class B cow trail![4] Much of the traffic was confined to sea-lanes. A modern visitor who stepped back into fifth-century Ireland would observe random, shifting rural sprawl in every direction.

Patrick's successors adopted his principle of indigenous Christianity and extended it. They learned about monasteries from Eastern Christianity, perhaps through visits to Gaul and the Eastern church, and certainly through reading Athanasius's best-selling *Life of St. Anthony*. Then they substantially adapted the idea of the monastery to Ireland. The resulting community was different enough from the Eastern monastery that we need a distinct term, such as *monastic community*.

What was the difference between Eastern monasteries and Celtic monastic communities? Briefly, the Eastern monasteries organized to protest, and escape from, the materialism of the Roman world and the corruption of the Church; the Celtic monasteries organized to penetrate the pagan world and to extend the Church. The Eastern monks often withdrew from the world into monasteries to save and cultivate their own souls; Celtic leaders often organized monastic communities to save other people's souls. The leaders of the Eastern monasteries located their monasteries in isolated locations, off the beaten track; the Celtic Christians typically built their monastic communities in locations accessible to the traffic of the time, such as proximity to settlements, on hilltops, or on islands near the established sea-lanes.[5]

Celtic monastic communities did include some monks and/or nuns who lived disciplined ascetic lives. Such monks and nuns often founded monastic communities, but Celtic communities were much more diverse than Eastern monasteries. Priests, teachers, scholars, craftsmen, artists, cooks, farmers, families, and children, as well as monks and/or nuns—all under the leadership of a lay abbot or abbess—populated the communities.[6] They had little use for more than a handful of ordained priests, or for people seeking ordination; they were essentially lay movements. More than a thousand people lived in some monastic communities. A few, such as Bangor and Clonfert, may have been as large as three thousand people.

Within the threefold division of the day into worship, study, and work, monastic communities were beehives of a wide range of activities. John Finney observes that "there would have been little of the monastic peace that pervades modern communities and [the] monks went outside the enclosure when they wanted peace and quiet."[7] With some variation from one community to another, children went to school, young men and women prepared for Christian vocations, and Christian scholarship was fostered.[8] Some inhabitants copied decaying books onto new parchments, others "illuminated" the Scriptures, and others practiced other arts and crafts.[9] Other people herded cows, sheared sheep, made cloth, cultivated crops, cooked for the community, or cared for sick people, sick animals, or guests. The community worshiped together, perhaps twice daily; they learned much of the Scriptures together—by heart—especially the Psalms. They nourished one another in a life of "contemplative prayer," and many monastic communities primarily functioned as "mission stations," preparing people for ministry to pre-Christian populations.[10]

Some ways in which a Celtic monastic community differed from an Eastern cloistered monastery would have been obvious to any sojourner. The visitor would first pass beyond a circular outer wall and through a gate that signified one was entering hallowed ground. The wall did not signify an enclosure to keep out the world; the area signified the "alternative" way of life, free of aggression and violence and devoted to God's purposes, that the community modeled for the world. Philip Sheldrake tells us:

> This enclosure, or termon, was to be a place free from all aggression. Violence was legally and absolutely excluded by this precinct. . . . Monastic settlements [were] anticipations of paradise in which the forces of division, violence and evil were excluded. Wild beasts were tamed and nature was regulated. The privileges of Adam and Eve in Eden,

received from God but lost by the fall, were reclaimed. The living out of this vision of an alternative world involved all the people who were brought within the enclosed space.[11]

Once past the enclosure, the visitor would notice (say, as at Glendalough) a porter's dwelling, a cathedral, several chapels, a round tower, one or more tall stone Celtic crosses, a cemetery, a well, the abbot's house, a guesthouse, many small cells for one or two people, larger dwellings for families, a kitchen, a refectory, a scriptorium, a library, workshops, farmland, grazing land, and so on. The visitor would especially notice the guesthouse. Sheldrake informs us that

> guests . . . were accorded a kind of semi-spiritual status and housed within the sacred enclosure. Often the guest house was given the choicest site within the settlement and yet was always set apart, sometimes within its own enclosure. The hospitium, therefore, was within the sacred space (isolated from the outside world) yet separated from the monastic living quarters. The guest facility was itself, therefore, a kind of "boundary place" between two worlds.[12]

The geography and architecture of the monastic community would appear quite planned and organized—in two or more concentric circles. The perceptive visitor would appreciate that the Celtic Christian movement had created community in the midst of rural sprawl!

There are two ways (at least) in which these communities produced an exceptional approach to the living out of Christianity, compared to the Roman form on the Continent. First, the monastic communities produced a less individualistic and more community-oriented approach to the Christian life. This affected the way in which—in churches, settlements, tribes, and families—the people supported one another, pulled together, prayed for one another, worked out their salvation together, and lived out the

Christian life together. Every person had multiple role models for living as a Christian, and in a more profound and pervasive sense than on the Continent, Irish Christians knew what it meant to be a Christian family or tribe. (Chapter 4 expands upon the Celtic movement's communal approach to Christianity.)

Second, Celtic Christianity addressed a "zone" of human concern that Western Christianity had generally ignored. Paul Hiebert's classic article "The Flaw of the Excluded Middle" shows how the earth's peoples explain life, live life, and face the future at three levels.[13]

The bottom level deals with the features in life that our senses can directly apprehend. At this level, people learn to plant a crop, to clean a fish, to fix a water pump, to build a house, and to do a thousand other things. This bottom level includes the "empirical" world that the sciences deal with.

The top level deals with the ultimate issues in life that are quite beyond what our senses can perceive; this is a "transcendent" or "sacred" realm that Christianity (and the other "world religions") usually address. Hiebert reports that "religion as a system of explanation deals with the ultimate questions of the origin, purpose, and destiny of an individual, a society, and the universe."[14] Hiebert observes that Western society and the Western churches have typically abandoned the bottom level to "common sense" and, in their fascination with the big metaphysical issues, have typically ignored the "middle level" that is nevertheless quite real to people in most societies (and increasingly real to postmodern people in the West).

What are the middle-level issues of life? Many people live much of their life anxious about the near future, the crises of their present life, and even the unknowns of the past. To be specific, the mother whose son faces a court trial, the laid-off father who cannot make the mortgage payment, the teen who experiences new hormones surging within him, and the woman who still struggles with the memory that a parent loved her sibling more are primarily driven at this middle level. Of these three dimensions—past, present, and near future—concerns about the near future hound many people much of the time. Although we know that seeds once planted should grow and bear fruit, that investments should provide for retirement, and that travel down this river on a boat (or down this highway in a minivan) should bring one to the destination, the future is not totally predictable. Accidents, misfortunes, the intervention of other persons, and other unknown events can frustrate human planning.[15]

For many peoples, Hiebert adds, this middle realm is inhabited by "mechanical" forces, such as mana, spells, omens, the evil eye, or luck, and/or by more "organic" presences, such as spirits, ghosts, ancestors, angels, demons, lesser gods, and so on. In their traditional folk religions, people turn to, say, the local shaman (who may be able to influence these middle-level forces) for a fruitful marriage, safety during travel, or protection from the evil eye or bad luck.[16]

The problem is that Western Christianity usually ignores this middle level that drives many people's lives much of the time. Western Christian leaders usually focus on the "ultimate" issues, as they define them, to the exclusion of the lesser issues; indeed, they often consider middle issues as beneath what they were educated and ordained to address! When Christianity ignores or does not help people cope with these middle issues, we often observe split-level Christianity in which people go to church so they can go to heaven but they also visit the shaman or the astrologer for help with what they are facing next week.

Celtic Christians had no need to seek out a shaman. Their Christian faith and community addressed life as a whole and may have addressed the middle level as specifically, comprehensively, and powerfully as any Christian movement ever has. A folk Christianity of, by, and for the people developed. It helped common people live and cope as Christians day by day in the face of poverty, enemies, evil forces, nature's uncertainties, and frequent threats from many quarters. This folk Christianity can be seen today in the people's prayers and blessings that were passed on orally for many generations. In the nineteenth century, Douglas Hyde interviewed many keepers of the Christian folk tradition in Ireland, and Alexander Carmichael collected such lore in the Hebrides Islands off Scotland's west coast. Carmichael's *Carmina Gadelica* was originally published in five volumes.[17] Reading through the *Carmina Gadelica* gives the reader a deep appreciation of the contemplative prayer that characterized Celtic Christian folk piety.

In *Exploring Celtic Spirituality*, Ray Simpson explains that episodic contemplative prayer, throughout the day, contrasts with the more standard ritual approach of praying at a specific time, place, or meeting, and it contrasts with the more usual petitionary approach that "requests God to do specific things." Indeed, he observes, it is "the opposite of controlling prayer." Contemplative prayer is the way we fulfill Paul's counsel to "pray without ceasing."[18] It is an ongoing, or very frequent, opening of the heart to the triune God, often while engaging in each of the many experiences that fill a day.

The *Carmina Gadelica* tradition gave people brief daily rituals, which they learned more or less by heart, with suggested affirmations or prayers for directing their hearts, moment by moment, setting by setting. The Celtic Christians learned prayers to accompany getting up in the morning, dressing, starting the morning fire, bathing or washing clothes or dishes, "smooring" the fire at day's end, and going to bed at night. One for starting the morning fire begins,

> I will kindle my fire this morning
> In presence of the holy angels of heaven,
> God, kindle Thou in my heart within
> A flame of love to my neighbor,
> To my foe, to my friend, to my kindred all,
> To the brave, to the knave, to the thrall.[19]

The *Carmina Gadelica* taught people how to pray for sowing seed and harvesting crops; for herding cows, milking cows, or churning butter; for before a meal and after; for a sprain or a toothache; for a new baby or a new baby chick. Celtic Christians prayed while weaving, hunting, fishing, cooking, or traveling. They knew prayers for the healing of many conditions, including blindness, warts, bruises, swollen breasts, and chest seizures.

The *Carmina Gadelica* taught Celtic parents lullabies to sing to their children at night. It gave people affirmations to prepare themselves for prayer, such as,

> I am bending my knee
> In the eye of the Father who created me,
> In the eye of the Son who purchased me,
> In the eye of the Spirit who cleansed me,
> In friendship and affection.[20]

Many invocations, prayers, and blessings in the *Carmina Gadelica* employ repetition and are thoroughly trinitarian, as in the following prayer:

> I lie down this night with God,
> And God will lie down with me;
> I lie down this night with Christ,
> And Christ will lie down with me;
> I lie down this night with the Spirit,
> And the Spirit will lie down with me;
> God and Christ and the Spirit
> Be lying down with me.[21]

As we explore more thoroughly in chapter 4, the Celtic style of prayer engages people's imaginations through visual and spatial imagery:

> The Three Who are over me,
> The Three Who are below me,
> The Three Who are above me here,
> The Three Who are above me yonder;
> The Three Who are in the earth,
> The Three Who are in the air,
> The Three Who are in the heavens,
> The Three Who are in the great pouring sea.[22]

Many situations in the *Carmina Gadelica* are, of course, dated. Today, most people never smoor a fire or churn butter or shear sheep. Ray Simpson, in *Celtic Blessings for Everyday Life*,[23] has updated the Celtic contemplative prayer approach for this generation. For instance, Simpson has prayers for when one gets a new car, a bicycle, a motorcycle, or a new job. There are prayers for journeying by car or for working at one's computer. One finds prayers for the transitions of life—going to school, leaving school, leaving home, falling in love, undergoing a midlife crisis, and entering retirement. He features prayers for anniversaries and reunions, for divorce, for infertility and miscarriage, for stepchildren, and for battered people and victims of crime. Simpson even includes a prayer for taking an exam!

> *Exams*
> I bless this exam
> in the name of the Designer of truth.
> I bless this exam
> in the name of the Protector from ill.
> I bless this exam
> in the name of the Spirit who guides.
> Open my eyes to see how this subject
> reflects something of you.

Aid me to understand this subject
with my heart as well as with my head.
Give me
Wisdom to know the nub of things,
Strength to recall what is useful,
Peace to leave the result to you.[24]

The Celtic Christian movement multiplied mission-sending monastic communities, which developed and deployed teams into settlements to multiply churches and to start people in the life of full devotion to the triune God. This movement was fueled by "the burning zeal of the apostles of the country," and "their aim was wonderfully furthered by the ardent temperament of the newly won converts."[25] In two or three generations, all of Ireland had become substantially Christian, and as we will see in the next chapter, Celtic monastic communities became the strategic "mission stations" from which apostolic bands reached the "barbarians" of Scotland, much of England, and much of western Europe.

CHAPTER 3

To the Picts, the Anglo-Saxons, and Other "Barbarians"

ithin a century after Patrick's death, Irish Celtic Christians were lifting their eyes to see harvests beyond Ireland. In A.D. 563, an entourage accompanied Columba,[1] a formidable apostolic leader, to Iona, an island off the coast of southwest Scotland, which would serve as the primary base for reaching the Picts of Scotland. The size of his entourage—twenty bishops, forty priests, thirty deacons, and fifty students—suggests his seriousness.[2] Again, with appropriate adaptations for reaching people of a somewhat different culture, Celtic Christian leaders paid the price to understand the Picts, their language, and their culture; they multiplied monastic communities that sent out teams to engage settlements and plant churches. Within a century, the Picts were substantially Christian.

By the early seventh century, the demographics of northern and central England had changed. Swarms of Angles, Saxons, Jutes, and other Germanic peoples (known collectively as "Anglo-Saxons") invaded the land and drove many of the Britons to Brittany (where they became known as "Bretons") or to Wales (where they became known as the "Welsh"). The Britons who stayed were absorbed into Anglo-Saxon culture. In 633, Iona commissioned an entourage led by Aidan to establish a monastic community on a tidal island called Lindisfarne, off the coast of northeast England. Ian Bradley observes that Aidan's community "was to prove almost as important a missionary centre as its mother house at Iona. From it monks penetrated far down into the areas of England held by the pagan Angles and Saxons."[3]

The mission of Aidan and his people represented the third major strategic adjustment in the history of Celtic Christian expansion. Patrick and his people, who were Romanized Britons from England, had adapted their mission to fit the culture of the pagan Irish Celts. Columba and his people, all Irish, had adjusted to the somewhat different language and culture of the Celtic Picts in Scotland. Now Aidan and his entourage, most of them Irish, were in cross-cultural mission to the Germanic Anglo-Saxons now populating England—people with multiple (but similar) languages, cultures, and primal religions. Henry Mayr-Harting explains, "As all the Germanic peoples had issued ultimately from Scandinavia, so they shared a common stock of mythology with the Scandinavians."[4] Again, the missionaries labored to understand these very different populations.

In broad outline, the emerging strategy of Aidan and his people looks familiar. First, they multiplied monastic communities. We have no way of knowing how many such communities the movements spawned by Patrick, Columba, Aidan, and others established in the British Isles alone. John Finney cites evidence showing thirty-two monastic communities in the area of Worcester; that density would indicate many hundreds of monastic communities across the British Isles.[5]

Second, the monastic communities sent apostolic teams to reach settlements within the region. Finney observes that an abbot or abbess often led the monastic community; a bishop often led the apostolic team. In the Celtic Christian movement, "the bishops performed the sacramental actions peculiar to their order, such as ordination, but above all were the leaders of evangelistic missions into the surrounding countryside and to the local secular leader-ship."[6] The team would engage in sustained group visits to settlements where they would minister with the people, interpret the gospel in indigenous ways, and plant churches. Aidan and his people were able to build on the efforts of Paulinus (and others) who preceded them in Northumbria.[7] Nevertheless, the Anglo-Saxons were not reached easily. Mayr-Harting reports:

> The Anglo-Saxons . . . were not converted at all quickly. . . . It took nearly 90 years to convert just the kings and the greater part of their aristocracy, not to speak of the country-side which was a question of centuries. In the course of that near-90 years, hardly a court was converted which did not suffer at least one subsequent relapse into paganism before being reconverted.[8]

Meanwhile, in this same period, another mission was launched in the south of England, at Canterbury. Pope Gregory, with a vision to make "angels" of the "Angles," commissioned a librarian named Augustine and forty other monks to England. These missionaries of the Roman Chris-tian tradition arrived in 597, and in time their movement experienced some success. Essentially, they succeeded in reaching several peoples in the south of England, largely south of the Thames.[9] The Roman tradition regards Augus-tine as "The Apostle of England." While Augustine's work began in 597, and Aidan's not until 633, the movement of Aidan expanded so much more and reached so many of the peoples of northern and central England that a stronger case can be made for Aidan being "The Apostle of Eng-land." (Occasionally writers, from Bede in the eighth cen-tury to Douglas Meek in the twentieth, have asserted that Augustine's mission was more significant than Aidan's or even Patrick's! Both writers assumed that culturally Roman patterns of Christianity's expressions should have been imposed everywhere and that the Celtic movement should have conformed to Roman ways and not indulged in contextualized expressions of the faith. Unless one agrees that culturally Roman Christianity was the only form worth spreading, however, Augustine's achievement, while important, inspiring, and instructive, pales in comparison.)

In the period in which England's demographics were changing because of the Anglo-Saxon occupation, the demographics of western Europe were changing even more. "Barbarian" Germanic populations like the Goths had pressured and invaded the Roman Empire for decades while, from multiple causes, the empire was also crumbling from within.[10] Rome itself fell to a military invasion in 410, and a series of events occurred that would, in time, usher in the Dark Ages—in which the "barbarian" hordes largely destroyed the arts, architecture, and (especially) the libraries of Roman civilization.

Meanwhile, back in Ireland, the Irish Christian leaders were convinced that they had learned something about reaching barbarians. Indeed, they now believed they were a people chosen by God for mission to the barbarians of western Europe. An Irish apostle named Columbanus, with an entourage, departed for Europe in 600 to launch a Celtic Christian mission to the Continent. He may not have been the first Irish apostle to Europe, "but he was certainly the pioneer who inspired the mass exodus later."[11] Irish missionaries in Europe faced the threefold challenge of converting barbarian peoples to Christianity, converting Arian Christians to orthodox Christianity, and renewing Christian populations that had "fallen into laxity and immorality."[12]

In the next fifteen years, Columbanus founded monastic communities in what is now France, Switzerland, and Italy; in time his people founded a vast network of sixty or more monastic communities, learned a dozen or more languages and cultures, engaged peoples, planted churches, and launched a significant Christian movement among the barbarian peoples of Europe, particularly in what is now France, Belgium, Switzerland, Austria, Germany, and Italy. In the first half of the eighth century, Boniface—an Anglo-Saxon mission leader employing (more or less) Celtic methods of mission—provided an additional generation of leadership that, in time, enabled the Germanic peoples of Europe to become substantially Christian.

Through several generations of sustained mission, Celtic Christianity thus re-evangelized Europe, helped bring Europe out of the Dark Ages, fueled Charlemagne's Carolingian Renaissance, and ushered in the Holy Roman Empire. Even those Celtic Christians who did not venture out but stayed at the monasteries played an indispensable role. By laboring in their scriptoria to copy the learning of the past onto new parchment, they preserved for posterity much of the classic literature of Christianity and of Greece and Rome. That, in the words of Thomas Cahill, is "how the Irish saved civilization!" While the Roman branch of the Church had long stopped growing, the mission of the Celtic branch had rescued Western civilization and restored movemental Christianity in Europe. Their achievement *should* have settled an old issue; they demonstrated that Christianization encourages, advances, and even restores civilization.

You would think that the politically dominant Roman wing of the Church would have been grateful for the expansion achieved by the mission of the Celtic wing, and begrudgingly, it was; but the Roman wing's leaders repeatedly criticized the Celtic wing for not doing church the Roman way! The two wings of the Church came into focused conflict at the Synod of Whitby in 664, called by the regional King Oswiu.[13] They clashed over two apparently superficial issues: (1) By their contrasting method of calculating the date for Easter, the Celtic churches were often celebrating Easter on a different date than Rome prescribed;

and (2) the hairstyle of the Celtic priests and monks contrasted with the "tonsure" of Roman priests and monks. The two sides expounded their views at the Synod of Whitby. The Romans arrived better organized, and once again, the lions defeated the tigers. King Oswiu sided with the Roman case and ruled that the Roman approach should replace the Celtic approach everywhere. In 670, a synod at Autun in France ruled that the Celtic monastic communities across Europe had to adopt the (Roman) Benedictine Rule.[14]

The real issues, of course, ran deeper than hairstyle, a date for Easter, and norms for community life. One issue was conservatism versus change. The Celtic Christians used a more ancient method for calculating the date of Easter than did the Romans; in that practice, and many others, they had not adopted Rome's innovations. David Bosch observed, "By and large, . . . Catholicism endorsed the principle that a 'missionary church' must reflect in every detail the Roman custom of the moment."[15]

A second issue was indigeneity versus cultural uniformity. In the hairstyle matter and many others, Celtic Christianity had adapted to the people's culture; the Romans wanted Roman cultural forms imposed upon all churches and peoples—a policy that was alien to the Celtic movement's practice and genius.

The third (and driving) issue, of course, was control and conformity. That is why it was so important to the Romans that everyone to do church the Roman way. Once any society accepted Christianity, the politically dominant Roman wing of the church insisted that the young churches organize in the Roman pattern of dioceses led by bishops and learn to worship in Latin, follow the liturgy from Rome, sing the music from Rome, and so forth.

The Synods of Whitby and Autun presumably settled the matter: the Roman way should be followed everywhere. In some cases, Celtic priests who refused to do church the

Roman way were banished; in other cases, Benedictine Rule was forced on Celtic monasteries.[16] More often, presumably, church and secular leaders simply pressured Celtic leaders to conform, and they praised and rewarded those who did. Within two centuries of the Synods at Whitby and Autun, the Roman way largely prevailed throughout the Western church. Nora Chadwick observes that

> the disappearance of the idiosyncratic Christianity of the Celtic Church was inevitable, owing to the absence of central organization; but it is impossible to reach the end without a feeling of regret. A Christianity so pure and so serene as that of the age of the saints could hardly be equaled and never repeated.[17]

Bede's history of the monasteries at Wearmouth and Jarrow, in northeast England, is a local edition of this wider history.[18] Bede's version of this local history begins with the story of the abbot Benedict, who

> went to Rome, where, in fulfillment of his long and ardent desire, he made sure he visited the tombs of the apostles and venerated their remains. Directly he returned home he devoted himself wholeheartedly and unceasingly to making known as widely as possible the forms of church life, which he had seen in Rome and had come to love and cherish.[19]

Doing church the Roman way was Benedict's obsession (and, transparently, Bede's as well). Bede's history of the two monasteries reports frequent travel, by abbots and monks, to and from Rome. They visited shrines in Rome, they observed how churches in Rome were doing church, and they sent their bishop to be consecrated in Rome. They stocked their libraries with books from Rome. They brought paintings and sacred relics from Rome. They built a "stone church in the Roman style."[20] At one point, Benedict brought from Rome a choirmaster named John who "taught the monks at first hand how things were done in the churches in Rome."[21]

For the record, Bede and the other Roman Christian leaders were not prejudicial toward Celtic culture only, nor were they engaged in selective discrimination against Celtic ways; they assumed that Roman ways were superior to the ways of all other cultures. Furthermore, they were supremely confident that Christianity could be adequately expressed only in the Latin language and in Roman cultural forms.

One case reveals these convictions with irrefutable clarity. Bede reports an event in which the pope consecrated Theodore, a Greek, to serve as a bishop in Britain.[22] An abbot, Hadrian, was assigned to accompany, coach, and mentor Theodore until he had internalized Roman ways. The purpose of Hadrian's assignment was to "take special care that Theodore should not, according to the custom of the Greeks, introduce anything contrary to the true faith into the church where he presided."[23]

So Bede reports and applauds, ad nauseam, the ways in which the monasteries of Wearmouth and Jarrow learned to do everything as in Rome. The rule had changed from "When in Rome, do as the Romans do" to "When you are anywhere, do as the Romans do!" Notice that, by Bede's account, neither Wearmouth nor Jarrow engaged in any mission to pagan populations or in any ministry or witness to seekers outside or inside either monastery. Wearmouth and Jarrow adopted the Roman forms and the Eastern agenda; their monks experienced the community's Roman ways in order to save their own souls.

Something like the Wearmouth and Jarrow experiences took place almost everywhere and, almost everywhere, the more Roman the monastic communities and churches became, the less they engaged in evangelization. Consequently, the Celtic church became history, although cultural enclaves of Celtic folk Christianity have continued in areas of Ireland, Wales, Cornwall, Scotland, and the Hebrides Islands until today. But the heroic Celtic era of mission eventually ended, and Christianity's apostolic mission was negligible for centuries—until its revival, half a millennium later, in the Counter-Reformation. Not until the Renaissance and Reformation would indigenous languages, cultures, and religious expressions resurface across Europe. Not until Vatican II (1962–1965) would the Roman Catholic Church affirm the idea of indigenous Christianity.

Throughout Bede's *Ecclesiastical History*, the nongrowing (Roman) wing of the Church always assumed that it knew better than the growing (Celtic) wing, and the nongrowing wing worked overtime to control the growing wing and make it conform. By the time the nongrowing wing succeeded in dominating the growing wing, however, the latter had reached the West for a second time.

I have reported at length on the ancient Roman ecclesiastical campaign to control the growing Celtic movement because we observe a parallel case today in most of the mainline denominations of the United States, especially those denominations once born in Europe and historically exported to North America.

In most American denominations, including mine, the people who control the denomination (or at least control the agenda of the denomination) are the same people who are less apostolic in their emphasis, who assume that they know best, who put in the most overtime to gain and retain influence in the denomination, and who are certain that a European way of doing church is best for all churches. Their special obsession is to control the growing wing of the church and "correct" it in a European direction! (The model has shifted in one important way. A thousand years ago, Church executives pressured churches to do church in current ways that reflected the Roman customs of the moment. Today, executives expect the churches to do church in traditional European ways while complying with the hierarchy's political views of the moment!)

For many decades, a European model for American churches was reasonably effective because the United States moved through history more or less in tandem with Europe until, say, the 1920s—when western Europe and North America moved increasingly in different directions. Today, as Lyle Schaller has demonstrated, virtually all denominations "imported from Europe" are declining while virtually all denominations "made in America" are growing.[24]

Why that should make a significant difference may not be obvious, but is easily demonstrated. For example, the architecture of an "imported from Europe" (IFE) church is often High Church Western European; the architecture of a "made in America" (MIA) church is usually functional and open. IFE liturgical language is usually rooted in the European past; MIA liturgical language is usually current American English. IFE beliefs and worship traditions usually emphasize the First Person of the Trinity; MIA beliefs and worship traditions usually emphasize the Second or Third Person of the Trinity.

More specifically, IFE churches usually feature acoustic sounds and music composed before 1960 (or 1760!); MIA churches are more likely to feature electronic sounds and music composed after 1960 (or 1990). The worship of IFE churches is usually formal, developed for believers, with the goal of "proper worship"; the worship of MIA churches is more likely to be informal, developed with seekers in mind, with the goals of meeting people's religious needs and changing lives.

IFE denominations usually have a hierarchical organization, which produces programs for the churches and expects people to trust the system; MIA denominations more likely have a flatter organization, which works more responsively with churches and expects the system to trust the people. IFE churches usually think of the church as the real estate and have low expectations of the members; MIA churches more often think of the church as the people and have high expectations of the members. Churches made in America are much more likely to give people choices, to be future oriented, to affirm entrepreneurs and new ideas, and to start new ministries and new churches than churches imported from Europe.[25] In other words, the Protestant Reformation left the control-from-Rome paradigm essentially unchallenged. For Protestants, the locus of control merely shifted from Rome to Wittenberg or Geneva or Canterbury, and then to New York or Chicago or Nashville. Most of the Europe-oriented leaders of America's mainline denominations are in denial, however, and they continue to assume that control from headquarters and the culturally European paradigm are best for all churches, everywhere.

As I was finishing the first edition of this book, these very issues surfaced in the 1998 meeting of the World Council of Churches in Harare, Zimbabwe. Christianity is now growing rapidly in Africa; Roman Catholicism doubled in twenty years; Lutherans grew by two-thirds in seven years. However, the continual pressure for African churches to do church in European (and American) ways has caused the rise of many African Independent Churches, who insist on the right to do church in African ways for Africans, and who are now growing much more than the African denominations still tied to Euro-American denominations. In the Harare meeting, however, African theologians (!) advocated more culturally African ways for Africans, claiming that worship should engage Africans emotionally as well as intellectually. They observed that many "churches have grown by embracing African forms of worship, sacred music and dance, and by moving away from styles linked with former colonial rulers."[26]

CHAPTER 4

The Celtic Christian Community in Formation and Mission

hat can now be known about how Celtic Christianity "won the West" for the second time? The rest of this book unpacks the multiple known strategic causes for Celtic Christian expansion. This chapter focuses on how the Celtic way of being and doing church contributed to the re-evangelization of Europe in the centuries before the Roman way eclipsed the Celtic way. Five themes suggest what we might learn from the ancient Celtic Christian movement about actually being the kind of missional church that many leaders now discuss.

First, in significant contrast to contemporary Christianity's well-known evangelism approaches of Lone Ranger one-to-one evangelism, confrontational evangelism, or the public preaching crusade (and in stark contrast to contemporary Christianity's more dominant "don't ask, don't tell" policy of not evangelizing at all!), we have already seen how the Celtic Christians usually evangelized as a team—by relating to the people of a settlement; identifying with the people; engaging in friendship, conversation, ministry, and witness—with the goal of raising up a church in measurable time. John Finney observes that the Celts believed in "the importance of the team. A group of people can pray and think together. They inspire and encourage each other. The single entrepreneur is too easily prey to self doubt and loss of vision."[1]

The second theme focuses on how the monastic community prepared people to live with depth, compassion, and power in mission. Celtic Christianity seems to have prepared people through a fivefold structure of experiences:

1. You experienced voluntary periods of solitary isolation, ordinarily in a primitive cell erected within a remote natural setting—like a grove of trees near a stream. Drawing on the wisdom of the desert fathers and mothers of the Eastern church, Celtic leaders advised you to "go, sit in your cell, and your cell will teach you everything."[2]

2. You spent time with your *anam cara*, that is, your "soul friend"—not a superior like a spiritual director, but more like a peer with whom you were voluntarily vulnerable and accountable; to whom you made confession; from whom you received penance; who both supported and challenged you.[3]

3. If the monastic community was at all large, you spent time with a small group of ten or fewer people—led by someone chosen primarily for his or her devotion.[4]

4. You participated in the common life, meals, work, learning, biblical recitation, prayers, ministries, and worship of the whole monastic community.

5. Through your small group and the community's life, and perhaps as a soul friend, you observed and gained experience in ministry and witness to pre-Christian people. The community's purposes for you, through this fivefold structure, were to root your consciousness in the gospel and the Scriptures; to help you experience the presence of the triune God and an empowered life; to help you discover and fulfill your vocation; and to give you experience in ministry with seekers.

A third theme, weaving through the second, focuses on the role of frequent imaginative prayer in all the settings (in solitude, with the soul friend, in the small group, in the corporate life, and in ministry with believers and seekers) of life within the monastic community. We will see, in chapter 5, that Celtic evangelization took people's "right brains" seriously; it made the gospel's meaning vivid, engaged people's emotions, and energized their response by engaging their imaginations.

The Celts' affirmation of human imagination also shaped the legendary Celtic life of private prayer. Esther de Waal is a contemporary champion of activating the religious imagination for meaningful prayer.[5] She defines the Christian life as a journey, in the company of other pilgrims and the triune God, with dark forces about us and the saints pulling for us. The imaginative style of prayer that fuels this life typically focuses on space and images, attains a visual quality, and is characterized by cogency and poetic repetition. De Waal explains:

> Above all the Celtic tradition has reminded me of the importance of images, those foundational images whose depths and universal character have always brought such riches to Christian understanding. . . . It now becomes vital, more than ever, to recover the fundamental images of fire, wind, bread, water, of light and dark, of the heart. These are the great impersonal symbols which are universal, understood by Christian and nonchristian alike.[6]

The Psalms, of course, have these features, and the people in a monastic community typically sang and prayed thirty psalms a day. However, the Celtic Christians also wrote new prayers, and many have been passed on for centuries. This part of a prayer serves as an example of cogency and poetic repetition:

O Father who sought me
O Son who bought me
O Holy Spirit who taught me.[7]

The most famous Celtic prayer, "St. Patrick's Breast-plate," stands as a magnificent example of the visual quality of many Celtic prayers:

I rise today
in power's strength, invoking the Trinity,
believing in threeness,
confessing the oneness,
of creation's Creator.

I rise today
in the power of Christ's birth and baptism,
in the power of his crucifixion and burial,
in the power of his rising and ascending,
in the power of his descending and judging.

I rise today
in the power of the love of cherubim,
in the obedience of angels,
and service of archangels,
in hope of rising to receive the reward,
in the prayers of patriarchs,
in the predictions of prophets,
in the preaching of apostles,
in the faith of confessors,
in the innocence of holy virgins,
in the deeds of the righteous.

I rise today
in heaven's might,
in sun's brightness,
in moon's radiance,
in fire's glory,
in lightning's quickness,

in wind's swiftness,
in sea's depth,
in earth's stability,
in rock's fixity.

I rise today
with the power of God to pilot me,
God's strength to sustain me,
God's wisdom to guide me,
God's eye to look ahead for me,
God's ear to hear me,
God's word to speak for me,
God's hand to protect me,
God's way before me,
God's shield to defend me,
God's host to deliver me:
from snares of devils,
from evil temptations,
from nature's failings,
from all who wish to harm me,
far or near,
alone and in a crowd.

Around me I gather today all these powers
against every cruel and merciless force
to attack my body and soul,
against the charms of false prophets,
the black laws of paganism,
the false laws of heretics
the deceptions of idolatry,
against spells cast by women, smiths and druids,
and all unlawful knowledge
that harms the body and soul.

May Christ protect me today
against poison and burning,
against drowning and wounding,
so that I may have abundant reward;
Christ with me, Christ before me, Christ behind me;

Christ within me, Christ beneath me, Christ above me,
Christ to right of me, Christ to left of me;
Christ in my lying, Christ in my sitting,
Christ in my rising;
Christ in the heart of all who think of me.
Christ on the tongue of all who speak to me,
Christ in the eye of all who see me,
Christ in the ear of all who hear me.

I rise today
in power's strength, invoking the Trinity,
believing in threeness,
confessing the oneness,
of creation's Creator.

For to the Lord belongs salvation,
and to the Lord belongs salvation
and to Christ belongs salvation
May your salvation, Lord, be with us always.[8]

The fourth theme is the role of the monastic community's hospitality in ministry with seekers, visitors, refugees, and other guests. We have already seen that one Celtic approach to pre-Christian people involved a team from the monastic community penetrating the natural community of the target population. We now feature a contrasting approach; the monastic communities invited seekers, refugees, and others, individuals and even families, to be their guests.

Put yourself in the place of a seeker, a refugee, or an abused teenager who has been invited to visit a monastic community, and you have found your way there. What would you likely experience?[9] You would meet a "porter" stationed near the monastic community's entrance, whose chief role is to welcome guests and introduce them to the rest of the community.[10] The abbot, and everyone else, would welcome you with "all courtesy of love." The abbot (or abbess) would gently inquire about what had prompted your visit (and so begin the ministry of conversation), would read a scripture for you, offer a prayer for you, and extend the "kiss of peace." The abbot would wash your feet (from your journey by foot) and would show you to the guesthouse—which would be managed by a caring brother who would give you bedding. You would be included at the abbot's table at meals; if the abbot was in a period of fasting, he would break the fast—for the abbot has no higher priority than ministry with guests. You would learn that the monastic community's highest commitment is hospitality to strangers, seekers, pilgrims, and refugees. The Benedictine Rule 53 mandates, "All guests who present themselves are to be welcomed as Christ, for he himself will say: 'I was a stranger and you welcomed me.'"

Soon you would be given a soul friend, a small group, and a place for periods of solitude. You would learn some Scripture; you would worship with the community. One or more persons would share the ministry of conversation and pray with you daily. After some days or weeks, you would find yourself believing what these Christians believe, and they would invite you to commit your life to Christ and his will for your life.

The fifth and final theme follows from the fourth and focuses more explicitly on the role of the seeker's experience of the Christian community in the process of conversion. This theme represents the major contribution of John Finney's pioneering book *Recovering the Past: Celtic and Roman Mission.*[11] Finney's book does us the service of contrasting the Roman way of doing mission and evangelism vis-à-vis the Celtic way.

Bluntly stated, the Roman model for reaching people (who are already "civilized" enough) is this: (1) present the Christian message; (2) invite them to decide to believe in Christ and become Christians; and (3) if they decide positively, welcome them into the church and its fellowship.

The Roman model seems very logical to us because most American Christians are scripted by it! We explain the gospel, they accept Christ, and we welcome them into the church. Presentation, decision, assimilation—what could be more logical than that?

But you already know enough to infer the (contrasting) Celtic model for reaching people: (1) establish community with people or bring them into the fellowship of your community of faith; (2) within fellowship, engage in conversation, ministry, prayer, and worship; and (3) in time, as they discover that they now believe, invite them to commit.

We can contrast the two models on a chart:

Roman Model	Celtic Model
Presentation	Fellowship
Decision	Ministry and conversation
Fellowship	Belief, invitation to commitment

The Celtic model reflects the adage that, for most people, "Christianity is more caught than taught!"

Years ago, I began discovering the Celtic approach in my field research with converts out of secularity into faith. In interviews, I usually ask new believers: "When did you feel that you really belonged, that you were wanted and welcomed and included in the fellowship of this church?" More and more converts, including a majority of boomer converts and a large majority of Generation X converts, comment that they felt like that before they believed and before they officially joined. Indeed, many new believers report that the experience of the fellowship made it possible for them to believe and commit. For many people, the faith is about three-fourths caught and one-fourth taught.

My cautious conclusions about how most people become Christians were reinforced by a more empirical study sponsored by the United Bible Societies in Great Britain, led and written by John Finney. A research team received 360

completed questionnaires from converts, and they interviewed 151 converts. These 511 converts represented the
range of denominations in England, from Anglican and
Roman Catholic, to "Free Churches" and the "New
Churches." In *Finding Faith Today: How Does It Happen?*[12]
Finney reports that most people experience the faith through
relationships, that they encounter the gospel through a community of faith, and that becoming a Christian involves a
process that takes time. In his later book *Recovering the Past*,
Finney summarizes their chief finding in four words. For
most people, "belonging comes before believing."

Finney believes that we are now rediscovering the
approach to mission first pioneered by ancient Celtic Christianity. He contends that the Celtic way is more effective
with postmodern Western populations than the Roman
way (and its more recent version—the traditional evangelical way). His data show that more people come to faith
gradually (the Celtic model) than suddenly (the Roman
model). Furthermore, the ongoing contagious common life
of the congregation that permits people to discover faith
for themselves, at their own pace, now appears to be much
more influential than special-event-preaching evangelism.
Finney outlines the typical journey of faith that most people experience today:[13]

1. X is introduced into the church through a member of
   his or her family, through friendship with some Christians, or through a minister.
2. He or she begins to ask questions.
3. He or she is invited to explore further and come to a
   knowledge and practice of the faith (often this is through
   a nurture group or some form of catechumenate).
4. The individual discovers that he or she has become a
   Christian and marks it publicly through baptism or
   confirmation or whatever is appropriate to his or her
   denomination.

If, as observed above, "belonging comes before believing," then evangelism is now about "helping people to belong so that they can believe." Finney believes that, as we adapt to a changing Western postmodern culture, we will observe a widespread shift from the entrenched Roman model to the rediscovered Celtic model.

CHAPTER 5

How Celtic Christianity Communicated the Gospel

We have seen that the Celtic monastic communities, and the apostolic teams from these communities, engaged and reached pre-Christian "barbarian" populations who typically had no prior knowledge of Christianity's message and who most Christian leaders assumed were unreachable. I have suggested that understanding the target populations was indispensable, that the people were more responsive when they sensed that Christians understood them, and that when seekers were welcomed into Christian fellowship, before they yet believed very much or experienced very much, the faith was even more caught than taught.

We now address this important question: how did the Celtic Christian movement *communicate* the gospel so effectively to the "barbarian" populations in Ireland, Scotland, England, and western Europe? Although "no one can say, 'Jesus is Lord' except by the Holy Spirit" (1 Corinthians 12:3), several perspectives in the field of communication theory enable us to perceive what the Celtic Christians were doing that helped communicate the meaning of the Christian message.

Aristotle, in his *Rhetoric*, which was published more than three centuries before Christ, observed effective (and ineffective) speakers in legislatures, law courts, and ceremonial settings, and he wrote the earliest comprehensive volume of rhetorical communication theory.[1] He defined rhetoric, essentially, as the study of competent public communication. He was interested in the most effective communicators' ability to discover and draw on the available means of influencing or persuading any audience, in any setting. He was especially interested in what the target audience already assumed, knew, or believed that the advocate could build on.

Aristotle observed that communication and persuasion take place in an interaction between the speaker, the message, and the audience, within a context, setting, or occasion. Although writers since Aristotle have often used other terms for the speaker (such as the *communicator* or *source*) and for the audience (such as the *receivers* or *receptors*), Aristotle's model has served as the prevailing model of the communication process for twenty-three centuries.

More specifically, Aristotle taught that public influence occurs from an interaction between the ethos of the communicator, the logos of the message, and the pathos of the audience.

I believe that much of the unusual communicative power of the Celtic Christian movement was attributable to the ethos of its communicators and its communities. Aristotle believed that when auditors hear an advocate speaking, they are asking (perhaps subconsciously) whether the speaker can be trusted and believed. Aristotle observed that, in complex matters—such as legislative proposals and court cases—in which even the community of experts cannot agree on what is true, the nonexpert public accepts "probability."[2] The public accepts the idea, case, or proposal that seems (to them) most probably true, and their judgment of the idea is influenced by their judgment of the idea's advocate; the advocate they perceive as most trustworthy and believable is probably communicating truth.

Aristotle's chief point was memorably expressed, much later, in the words of Ralph Waldo Emerson. Emerson defined *eloquence* as "the art of speaking what you mean and are," and he proposed, "The reason why anyone refuses his assent to your opinion, or his aid to your benevolent design, is in you. He refuses to accept you as a bringer of truth, because, though you think you have it, he feels that you have it not. You have not given him the authentic sign."[3]

Let's revisit someone in whom the Irish perceived "the authentic sign." Following his Macedonian call, we can reasonably infer that Patrick reentered Ireland with the most remarkable ethos of any missionary who ever undertook a frontier mission. Imagine the rumor that would have spread like wildfire across the Irish people's grapevines: "Our slave Patrick has returned, at great personal risk, loving us and telling us that the High God loves us." Many stories circulated that reflected his compassion and his understanding of the Irish and their instinctive trust in him, such as the following: "They brought him a sick woman who was with child. He baptized the son in the mother's womb, the amniotic fluid being the water of baptism. They buried her below the bank of the church enclosure."[4]

One critical incident reflects how contagious the rumors were about Patrick, and the profound ethos that his courageous return to Ireland had catalyzed in the people's minds. Patrick resolved, early in his mission, to return to the region where he once lived as a slave. He planned to pay the bond money for his ransom to Miliuc, now an old man, who had bought him from the slave traders; and he wanted to tell Miliuc about Jesus the Christ, who paid the ransom for Miliuc's freedom from sin and death. When Miliuc heard that Patrick was en route to see him, he locked himself inside his house and burned it down.[5]

Despite Patrick's high ethos, which undoubtedly assured him a hearing in many tribes, he never "had it made" in his mission to Ireland. The high regard in which many Irish people held him posed a threat to many Druids and to some tribal kings who opposed him, often with threats. His published *Confession* alludes to the ever-present possibility of imprisonment or re-enslavement, and to "the twelve dangers which threatened [his] life."[6] Often, he had to pay for "protection" as he traveled. Yet the apostle's willingness to endure continuing danger for his mission would have fueled "the authentic sign."

What is involved in "the authentic sign" for which audiences are attuned? What, specifically, are people looking for? Aristotle identified three principles in the communicator's ethos: intelligence, character, and goodwill. So, to be believed, the speaker must be perceived to be informed, knowledgeable, and competent in the subject matter, with a capacity for valid reasoning, good judgment, and wisdom. To be trusted, the speaker must be perceived as a person of honesty, virtue, and integrity. To be believed and trusted, the speaker needs to be perceived as "for" the audience, on their side, more concerned for the audience's welfare than for self-gain. The communicator's ethos is so crucial that Aristotle claimed it is "almost . . . the controlling factor in persuasion."[7]

Later research has uncovered additional components of the public communicator's ethos that are operative for many auditors, if not all. For example, we now know that some auditors need to experience a speaker's dynamism; they have to receive "energy" from the communicator to maintain their interest. A speaker who exudes energy seems to amplify the auditor's (positive or negative) perception of the speaker's intelligence, character, and motivation.[8]

Again, Aristotle focused only on the advocate's "intrinsic" ethos—the audience's appraisal of the speaker during the speech. Since Aristotle, many writers have demonstrated that "extrinsic" ethos is at least as important; that is, the speaker's reputation (and perhaps his or her organization's reputation) prior to the speech is also a factor. In religious discourse (which Aristotle did not study), Saint Augustine observed that the preacher's *life*, as known and perceived by the people, strongly influences their reception of the message. Patrick, for example, rode a wave of high (extrinsic) ethos as he entered each settlement, and his demeanor, life, and compassion within each settlement would have strengthened his high ethos in the people's eyes.

Helmut Thielicke, a renowned German theologian and preacher, identified credibility as an operative factor in a public communicator's ethos.[9] We live, he maintained, in an age of "paid propagandists" for causes ranging from consumer products to political candidates. In that context, hearers want to know whether this politician will deliver on her promises if elected. They want to know whether that sports star really uses the underarm deodorant he advertises, and whether it really transformed his social life, or whether he is just a paid propagandist for the brand. Thielicke observed, in twentieth-century Germany, that secular audiences were asking credibility-related questions about advocates for Christianity: do Christian speakers live by this religion they are asking us to buy, or are they just paid propagandists for the institutional church?

My interview research with secular people, over several decades, has confirmed the prominence of the credibility theme in secular people's inquiries about Christianity. Their inquiries usually take one (or more) of four specific forms. First, some people wonder whether we really believe what we say we believe. Second, some people do not doubt that we believe it; they wonder whether we live by it. Third, some people do not doubt that we believe it or live by it; they wonder whether it makes much difference in our lives! Fourth (and more recently), they wonder whether Christianity can make a difference in the world— as related to struggles around justice, reconciliation, peace, and nature's health. Often, if they perceive "the authentic sign" in the answers they experience, they become more open to what it means and could mean for them.

The final (known) factor related to ethos is identification; this factor relates to the communicator's ethos and also to a kind of relationship between the communicator and the receptors. The concept of identification has had two prominent champions: Søren Kierkegaard and Kenneth Burke. Identification is the deepest and most complex of our concepts related to the communicator's ethos. Kierkegaard and Burke each wrote several volumes devoted (in part) to this concept.

At its heart, identification refers to a closeness that members of an audience experience between themselves and the communicator. If, in the goodwill dimension, auditors ask, "Is the communicator for us?"— then in the identification dimension, they ask, "Is the communicator with us?" We limit our exploration of this idea to the insights from Kierkegaard and Burke that are reflected in what we know about communication within the spread of Celtic Christianity.

Burke, a twentieth-century Marxist rhetorical theorist, preferred the term *identification* to *persuasion* in his study of the rhetoric of human influence because identification suggests that the factors in public influence are partly unconscious. The communicator's purpose is to establish rapport and community with the receptors; influence comes through such shared images, feelings, attitudes, beliefs, values, and experiences that the communicator and the people experience "consubstantiality."[10] Through effective identification, alienation can be overcome, the speaker and the audience can share vicariously in each other's interests and experiences, and the audience may experience "transcendence" and may identify with the advocate's cause.

How does Burke's communicator build such rapport with an audience? Essentially, communicators achieve identification by understanding, adapting to, and identifying with their audiences. More specifically, communicators do this by identifying with some of the people's beliefs, attitudes, values, needs, issues, and struggles, and by speaking their language and communicating within their thought patterns. Burke proposes using music, visual symbols, and the setting to facilitate the experience of community. The speaker should involve the auditors in active thought or in anticipating what comes next. Mobilizing the people into group participation, like laughter or hand clapping, can build community.

Kierkegaard, the nineteenth-century Danish philosopher and theologian, also believed that identification is the means through which advocates influence people. He specifically addressed the "Christendom" problem—that is, many people who live in a "Christian country" believe in Christianity but do not live by it, they do not perceive the contradiction, and they live with the "illusion" that they are Christians! A "direct" approach to such people, Kierkegaard observed, arouses defensiveness and is counterproductive. So he recommended "indirect" communication approaches that engage people's imaginations, such as through narrative, that "wound from behind" and help people to "discover" truth. He exclaimed, "The method must be indirect. . . . All the old military science, all the apologetic and whatever goes with it, serves rather—candidly speaking—to betray the cause of Christianity. At every instant and at every point the tactics must be adapted to a fight which is waged against a conceit, an illusion."[11]

Some of Kierkegaard's strategies—such as employing an "ambiguity" in speech that requires people in denial to think—are more appropriate to his Christendom context (in which the people still know enough about Christianity to inform their thinking) than to either the pre-Christian contexts that the Celtic Christian movement usually faced or the post-Christian contexts we face increasingly in the West. In pre-Christian and in post-Christian contexts, the advocate cannot assume basic Christian knowledge in the minds of the audience, so clarity is a greater requirement for engaging most of the people. Nevertheless, storytelling and other appeals to the imagination are effective, even essential, with many pre-Christian and post-Christian populations, and a primary reliance on direct propositional speaking is seldom as effective as it should be anywhere.

The following suggestions from Kierkegaard should be useful in most apostolic settings. First, engage and speak rather personally to individuals, not as to an audience en masse. As William Warren Sweet once observed, "To personalize religion is to emotionalize it."[12] Second, speak concretely, even poetically and imaginatively, rather than in abstractions. Third, speak to yourself as well as to the auditors so that the speech has the effect of the audience "overhearing" the speaker addressing the speaker. Fourth, stress the possibility of what a person's life can become. If you tell stories of heroes of the faith, the goal is not for the people to admire the heroes (that is counterproductive) but to glimpse what their own lives can become. Fifth, reject all temptation to pressure people to decide now; respect their freedom and encourage their free response in measurable time.

Until the mid-1980s, rhetorical theory was rather limited in its capacity to inform approaches to Christianity's apostolic mission. That mission, after all, hopes to help people experience forgiveness, reconciliation, second birth, a new community, and a new life, worldview, and purpose. Because Aristotle confined his reflection to (comparatively) limited challenges—such as understanding what approaches help legislation pass and what approaches win legal cases—his insights do not advance our understanding of the approaches that help change people's identities and lives as much as we long sensed was possible. Although later theorists like Augustine, Erasmus, and George Campbell moved some in that direction, they mainly informed our preaching and teaching to people who already believed. The thought of Kierkegaard and Burke had obvious implications, but (to my knowledge) no one fully addressed the kinds of challenges that apostles face until two 1987 publications.

In that year, Walter Fisher's *Human Communication as Narration* was published.[13] Fisher, who taught at the University of Southern California, took issue with the long intellectual tradition, from the classical period through the Enlightenment and the age of science, which defined human beings as essentially rational creatures who make decisions based on the best arguments and make sense of their world through rational analysis. He contended, instead, that humans are "storytelling animals"; we make sense of our lives, and of history and the world, within story lines. We, therefore, communicate most effectively through narrative, especially when the communicator's story connects with the audience's own stories. People still respond to "good reasons," but their worldviews, gained through their socialization and their life stories, influence what they consider good reasons.

In Walter Fisher's perspective, not all stories are created equal; people "buy" some stories and not others. People are more likely to buy into a story *if* (1) it has "narrative coherence": the story is plausible, its pieces fit together, its characters act consistently, and it seems to "hang together." Moreover, (2) people are likely to buy the story if it passes the test of "narrative fidelity": the story has sufficient congruity with the hearers' experiences and stories, is relevant to their world, and "rings true." Fisher believed in the power of narrative because he observed that human beings have the capacity to accept, and create, new stories that illuminate their lives.

In that same year, Maurice Charland introduced a paradigm shift.[14] Public communication was no longer merely about getting one's meaning across without distortion or persuading an audience to reach a decision. Some communication creates (or "constitutes") new realities—in the sense that two people, through communication, constitute a new friendship, a ministry team constitutes a new church, or a constitutional convention creates a new nation. Charland's constitutive rhetoric built upon Burke's identification theory to explain the creation, the shared new identity, and the mobilization of the French movement in Quebec for national sovereignty.

In 1980, 45 percent of Quebec's people voted to withdraw from Canada and become a sovereign nation. Charland studied how their "white paper," their speeches, rallies, meetings, conversations, and their socializing experiences "rhetorically constituted" the people's new shared identity over time. He discovered that the *Quebecois* were not so much rationally persuaded to choose their new identity; their new identity formed within them over time, somewhat intuitively, somewhat unconsciously.

Building also upon Walter Fisher, Charland saw that narrative is indispensable in constituting a new community. The movement's famous white paper featured the *Quebecois* story that stretched back as early as 1760, along the Saint Lawrence River; as an expatriate people, "French by language, culture, and politics, this society had a soul, a way of life, traditions," and "a collective destiny." While the story was part fact and part fiction, it took on reality as people identified with the narrative and adopted it as their story.

Charland became clear that two steps are indispensable if constitutive rhetoric is to be effective: (1) One necessary step is "interpellation," that is, *calling* the audience in a way that expects and virtually requires response. (2) The people must begin *acting together*, in their social world, upon their emerging identity. As they respond, act together, and begin telling the story to others and inviting them to involvement, the story and its driving ideas come to order their world and their way of life. Charland adds that if constitutive rhetoric is truly transformational, it also proceeds at the aesthetic level and engages people's affections through such expressions as music, art, drama, and architecture.

One towering question remained. Many people already have a shared identity, but it may be dysfunctional, or it may restrain their hopes as a people. So what can we know about the kind of discourse that might *re*constitute a people? John C. Hammerback and Richard J. Jensen studied such an achievement in the collective identity of Mexican American migrant workers in the American Southwest. The people had long lived in poverty; farm owners and governments had often defeated their aspirations for a better life. The people had substantially lost their sense of dignity as a people and doubted whether they were even entitled to the same rights as other people.

The speaking and leadership of one man, Cesar Chavez, gradually (over two decades) catalyzed a new self-understanding, a new worldview, and a new, active hope within them, which in time led to the establishment of a successful farm workers' movement (and a labor union) and, in time, to new laws, new rights, and new lives. Hammerback and Jensen studied the career advocacy of Chavez, as a case study, to discover what is essentially involved in the kind of reconstitutive rhetoric that enables a population to adopt a changed identity and live a new way of life. Building on the contributions of Burke, Charland, Fisher, and others, Hammerback and Jensen delineate a three-part model of reconstitutive rhetoric.[15]

The theory's first feature is *the first persona*—Hammerback's term for the person whom the leader appears to be, and is experienced to be, in the target population's eyes. In reconstitutive discourse, the ethos of the communicator counts much more than in other genres of public communication. The communicator is experienced, profoundly, to identify with the people, their issues, and their hopes. The communicator's speaking fits the people's indigenous linguistic style and their ways of reasoning. Furthermore, the communicator declares, dramatizes, and even embodies a narrative in which the people can make sense of their stories and become involved in the new story.

The theory's second feature is *the substantive message*—Hammerback's term for the story, themes, ideas, reasons, and explanations that form the movement cognitively—with the important addition that the primary leader (and other leaders) are perceived to embody the message and live it out, and to model what it means and looks like to live by it. When the advocate is experienced to deeply identify with the message, auditors who identify with that speaker will be inclined to identify with the message. Indeed, when the highly trusted speaker is thought to virtually incarnate the message, and to live by it, the people experience this as a proof of the message's validity.

The theory's third feature is *the second persona*. Simply stated, the rhetor tells the people who they are "called" to be and can really become. In reconstitutive discourse, issues like "who you are," "how you can live," and "the action you must take to get there" are sometimes implied and sometimes explicit. Reconstitutive messages often feature a "portrait" of what the audience can be and what their lives can become. Hammerback and Jensen concur with Charland that in constitutive *and* reconstitutive rhetoric, "Burkean identification rather than neo-Aristotelian persuasion forms the cornerstone of the rhetorical act." In the movements in Quebec and in California, advocates "created rather than persuaded audiences. . . . To create audiences, . . . speeches and writings must rely heavily on the second persona."[16]

We can infer that Patrick spoke with sufficient dynamism to engage the Celtic people who were used to eloquent speakers and splendid storytellers; Patrick's results suggest that he competed effectively with their indigenous communicators. We know more than enough to be satisfied that his perceived intelligence, character, goodwill, and credibility contributed to the evangelization of thirty or more tribes.

Only with time did the extent to which Patrick identified with the Irish, and with his converts and churches, become obvious to the British church leaders back home and perhaps to him. However, by the later years of his twenty-eight-year ministry in Ireland, when he wrote his *Confession* and his one letter that has survived, Patrick had identified completely with the Irish. Thomas Cahill observes:

> His love for his adopted people shines through his writings, and it is not just a generalized "Christian" benevolence, but a love for individuals as they are. . . . He worries constantly for his people, not just for their spiritual but for their physical welfare. . . . Patrick has become an Irishman.[17]

Patrick's "Letter against the Soldiers of Coroticus"[18] was written to British "Christian" soldiers who had denied both the Christian identity and the real humanity of the Irish Christians that they had kidnapped and sold into slavery. In the letter, Patrick denounces the British slave traders as "dogs" and "fellow-citizens of the demons"; he uses his episcopal authority to excommunicate them from the Church, and he leaves no doubt about who are now his people: "He is no longer British or Roman, at all. When he cries out in his pain, 'Is it a shameful thing . . . that *we* have been born in Ireland?' we know that he has left the old civilization behind forever and has identified himself completely with the Irish."[19] So, from the case of Patrick of Ireland, we can appreciate the musing of Aristotle and Burke that, among the three modes of persuasion—ethos, logos, and pathos—ethos plus identification are essential in transformational communication.

In the generations after Patrick, the continued spread of Celtic Christianity is substantially attributable to the first persona ethos of the Celtic Christian leaders (and their communities). Unfortunately, the ancient biographers who were the most devoted to perpetuating the memories of the Celtic saints are not reliably useful for helping us understand today how their ethos fueled the spread of Christianity. Because, in the early medieval Western world, most writers of the lives of saints felt obligated to demonstrate that their hero was a saint—by the extravagant standards of the times. Two examples will show this.

Muirchu's "Life of St. Patrick" is a memorable celebration of the life and ministry of Patrick, which incorporates stories from early sources such as Patrick's *Confession* and Tirechan's "Account" along with other material.[20] Some of this material reflects our theme. A pagan swineherd named Dichu, for instance, misperceived Patrick and his party for robbers as they approached, and Dichu resolved to kill them: "But when he saw the face of St. Patrick the Lord changed his mind for the better, and Patrick preached the faith to him."[21]

Though Patrick's own writing had reported new births, new churches, and changed lives, he had not featured extraordinary miracles from his ministry. Muirchu does feature miracles, however, because he believes that "the Lord . . . confirmed [Patrick's] words by the miracles that followed."[22] In one incident, a Druid who opposed Patrick was raised into the air. When he fell, "he smashed his skull on a rock, and died right before them, and the heathen were afraid." The king became enraged and sent his army against Patrick, but a sudden earthquake destroyed many of the king's chariots, horses, and warriors. As the king and his remaining warriors still pursued Patrick, Patrick and his band disappeared before the king's eyes, and the king saw only deer before him.[23] In several accounts of Patrick's confrontations with Druids, Patrick causes liquid in a glass to freeze, snow to disappear, fields to be made barren, and Druid opponents to be struck dead. Following Patrick's death, his body mysteriously disappears—by Muirchu's embellished account.

The *Life of St. Columba* by Adomnan of Iona[24] is like Muirchu's "Life of St. Patrick," only more so. Virtually the entire burden of Adomnan's story is to establish Columba's sainthood in terms of three expectations. Adomnan believed that he had to demonstrate that Columba experienced many prophetic revelations (book 1), that he was the agent of many divine miracles (book 2), and that "angelic apparitions and certain phenomena of heavenly light [were] seen above the man of God" (book 3).[25] As Adomnan tells stories that substantiate these three claims, we can obviously infer insights about the saint's dynamism, character, goodwill, credibility, and even compassionate identification with the Picts to whom he and his people were sent. Yet on one rare occasion when Adomnan reports a slice of Columba's apostolic ministry to the Picts, he reports the conversion and baptizing of a Pictish household as a prologue to telling us that Columba raised one of the family's children from death: "At the saint's glorious word the soul returned to the body, and the boy that was dead opened his eyes and lived again."[26] So the literary champions of the Celtic apostles can teach us *something* about their ethos if we can distinguish insight from legend. We may learn more, however, from a writer who kept some distance from the Celtic Christian leaders. One such source stands out.

The venerable Bede was a persistent, even obsessional, champion of the Roman approach to Christianity vis-à-vis the Celtic approach and all other ways. So he substantially disagreed with, and criticized, the Celtic Christian leaders who celebrated Easter on the wrong Sunday, wore their hair wrong, and did church in a hundred ways that were not culturally Roman. Regarding one factor in ethos theory, Bede took a somewhat low view of the intelligence of the Celtic Christian leaders. Although "zealous in the cause of God," their observance of Easter on the wrong Sunday was "not altogether according to knowledge."[27] Yet Bede recognized the orthodox theology of the Celtic Christian leaders, and he was profoundly impressed, and moved, by the character and credibility of the Celtic saints and by their empathy for the populations they reached. For example, Bede reports on the achievement of Columba and his people in establishing Iona, multiplying monastic communities, and reaching the Picts of Scotland:

> Columba . . . converted that nation to the faith of Christ, by his preaching and example. . . . He left successors renowned for their continency, their love of God, and observance of monastic rules. It is true they followed uncertain rules in their observance of . . . Easter. . . . [They] practiced such works of piety and chastity as they could learn from the prophetical, evangelical, and apostolical writings.[28]

Bede describes at greater length the character, credibility, and incarnational ministry of Aidan, apostle to the Anglo-Saxons of northern England. While still in Iona, before he was sent to establish the Lindisfarne base from which to reach the English,

> [Aidan] left the clergy a most salutary example of abstinence or continence; it was the highest commendation of his doctrine, with all men, that he taught no otherwise than he and his followers had lived; for he neither sought nor loved any thing of this world, but delighted in distributing immediately among the poor whatsoever was given him by the kings or rich men of the world. He was wont to traverse both town and country on foot, never on horseback, unless compelled by some urgent necessity; and wherever in

his way he saw any, either rich or poor, he invited them, if infidels, to embrace the mystery of the faith or if they were believers, to strengthen them in the faith, and to stir them up by words and actions to alms and good works. . . . I have written thus much concerning the person and works of . . . Aidan, in no way commending or approving what he imperfectly understood in relation to the observance of Easter; . . . but, like an impartial historian . . . commending . . . his actions.[29]

Bede continues to commend Aidan for his love of peace, for his charity and a dozen other virtues, and for "his mind superior to anger and avarice. . . . But I do not praise or approve his not observing Easter at the proper time."[30]

Bede also affirmed the ethos of Saint Cuthbert, a successor to Aidan in leading the Celtic Christian expansion in England. While he saw much the same character and credibility in Cuthbert that he saw in Columba and Aidan, he was especially impressed by Cuthbert's identification with the most marginalized unreached people of Anglo-Saxon society:

He was wont chiefly to resort to those places, and preach in such villages, as being seated high up amid craggy mountains, were frightful to others to behold, and whose poverty and barbarity rendered them inaccessible to other teachers; which nevertheless he, having entirely devoted himself to that pious labor, did so industriously apply himself [that] . . . he would often stay a week, sometimes two or three, and sometimes a whole month, before he returned home, continuing among the mountains to summon that rustic people by his preaching and example to heavenly things.[31]

Bede also held a positive image of the several Celtic monastic communities that he knew something about. For instance, he commended the credibility of the large community of men and women at Whitby, founded and led by Saint Hilda: "After the example of the primitive church, no person was there rich, and none poor, all being in common to all, and none having any property."[32]

However, our assurance of the character, goodwill, and credibility of these communities depends much less upon the observations of historians than upon the circumstantial evidence from what they achieved and how. They reached one barbarian population after another by welcoming seekers, who were looking for the authentic sign, into the close fellowship of their monastic communities, where seekers closely observed how the Christians lived day after day. As seekers spent time with a Celtic Christian community, they typically discovered who they were now called to be, and they found themselves wanting that new identity and believing what the Christians taught. Indeed, the Celtic Christians undoubtedly discovered that the presence of seekers observing them for the authentic sign provided an additional incentive for living faithful lives.

Aristotle observed that people are much more likely to respond to a message if, in addition to understanding it, they experience the emotion that energizes an appropriate response. People are unlikely to take action from information and reasons alone. Thomas de Quincey, standing in Aristotle's tradition, compared a speech to a ship; to move the ship (the audience), you need both a rudder (understanding) and a sail (passion).[33] Aristotle taught that we arouse human emotions in other people indirectly—by describing the object, person, or situation that, when seen in their imaginations, stimulates the desired emotion. Much later, George Campbell was to connect emotions to motives and desires; when people see the possibility that some deep desire can be fulfilled (or frustrated), they respond emotionally. A third way that a communicator might arouse emotions is through the use of emotionally loaded language; but if the communicator is not granted high ethos, that tactic can backfire.

The Irish and the other Celtic peoples (but especially the Irish) were passionate people who experienced and expressed the full range of human emotions, and they typically based decisions on how they felt. We have already seen that the Romans viewed the Celtic emotional intensity and volatility as one sign that they were barbarians. This image has stuck over time. In the nineteenth century, England's Prime Minister Benjamin Disraeli characterized the Irish as a "wild, reckless, indolent, uncertain and superstitious race."[34] Thomas Cahill explains what drove the Irish emotional agenda:

> Fixity escaped these people, as in the end it escapes us all. They understood, as few have understood before or since, how fleeting life is and how pointless to try to hold on to things or people. They pursued the wondrous deed, the heroic gesture: fighting, f**king, drinking, art—poetry for intense emotion, the music that accompanied the heroic drinking with which each day ended. . . . All these are worth pursuit, and the first, especially, will bring the honor great souls seek. But in the midst of this furious swirl of energy lies a still point of detachment. . . . The face of the Dying Gaul speaks for them all: each one of us will die, naked and alone, on some battlefield not of our own choosing. . . . After the assassination of John F. Kennedy, Daniel Patrick Moynihan was heard to say that to be Irish is to know that in the end the world will break your heart.[35]

We do not know precisely how the apostles to the Celts engaged in emotional appeals because we have no transcripts, or even elaborate summaries, of their discourse to the pagans. We can infer four insights. First, apostles like Patrick "had to find a way of connecting his message to their deepest concerns."[36] You cannot engage people seriously without engaging their motivational and emotional agenda. Second, in contrast to the indifference of their capricious gods, the people discovered that their feelings mattered to the triune God of Christianity. Third, their experience of God's providence gave them victory over terror and other destructive emotions. Fourth, Christianity gave them outlets for expressing their constructive emotions through indigenous oratory, storytelling, poetry, music, dance, drama, and so on in God's service. So, the Celtic Christian movement was effective, in part, because its leaders took the pathos of the Celtic audience seriously.

We have seen that much of the communicative power of the Celtic Christian movement was attributable to the ethos of its communicators, who affirmed and engaged the pathos of the Celtic audience. Turning now to the logos of the message, we see that while Patrick, Columba, Aidan, and the others could reason quite effectively with people, their genius (compared to the Romans) was in the imaginative communication of Christianity's message.

Several specific communication strategies (anticipated in the material from Burke and Kierkegaard, above) help account for the communicative effectiveness of the Celtic Christian movement. Each of these communication strategies represents one way to express the larger principle of imagination. Celtic Christianity took an imaginative approach to communicating the gospel mystery to barbarians. The early Celtic Chrisrtians tapped their own imaginations for fresh ways to communicate the good news, and they engaged the imaginations of pre-Christian seekers. Thomas Cahill tells us, "Patrick found a way of swimming down to the depths of the Irish psyche and warming and transforming Irish imagination—making it more humane and more noble while keeping it Irish."[37]

More than two centuries ago, a Scottish rhetorician named George Campbell elevated imagination to a prominent place in our understanding of the communication process, and subsequent history (as well as our study of prior history) has confirmed his judgment. In Campbell's theory, "to please the imagination" became one of the four goals in public communication,[38] and engaging people's imaginations is often a means of achieving any and all of the other three goals of speech—"to enlighten the understanding," "to move the passions," and "to influence the will." Writing in 1776, Campbell adhered to the faculty psychology school of thought instituted by Francis Bacon. Faculty psychologists believed that the human brain essentially functions in five ways—reasoning, feeling, imagining, remembering, and willing—and that these five "faculties" were rooted in distinct parts of the brain.

More recent research in brain anatomy has undermined Campbell's model, but the faculty psychologists nevertheless anticipated a model that now features the two hemispheres of the cerebrum. This model suggests that the left hemisphere controls the right side of the body, from which mental functions like speech, reasoning, and computation take place, while the right hemisphere controls the left side of the body, from which mental functions like imagination and artistic expression take place. Some people are predominantly "left-brained" analytical, and some people are predominantly "right-brained" artistic. Furthermore, some cultures are predominantly left-brained, and some are predominantly right-brained, and cultures can shift in their predominant orientation over time. In this theory, logical thinking, conceptualizing, and verbalizing are left-brained, "rational" activities, while intuiting, feeling, and imagining are right-brained, "experiential" activities. The following chart suggests some of the distinctions:[39]

Left Brain	Right Brain
Logic	Intuition
Concepts	Emotions
Abstraction	Imagination
Language	Art, music, poetry
Rational	Experience

Some mental activities, like remembering and willing, are undoubtedly rooted in both hemispheres of the brain. And, say, the writing of poetry or music employs both hemispheres.

The Irish and other Celtic peoples were predominantly right-brained, and in reaching them, Celtic Christianity adapted remarkably from its earlier Roman reliance upon words, propositions, concepts, and theological abstractions. Ian Bradley reports that Celtic Christianity was rooted even more in the imagination than the intellect and spoke in images more than in concepts. Celtic Christian leaders

> excelled at expressing their faith in symbols, metaphors and images, both visual and poetic. They had the ability to . . . paint pictures in words, signs and music that acted as icons opening windows on heaven and pathways to eternity. . . . They have much to teach Christians today seeking to rekindle their imaginative faculties.[40]

Celtic Christian communicators spoke from their imaginations to the imaginations of their hearers. They were less interested than the Church's Roman wing in apologetics— that is, rationally proving the validity of Christianity's truth claims. They seem to have believed that if you could make a Christian truth claim clear to the people's imaginations, the people and the Holy Spirit would take it from there, especially if they were already tasting Christian community. So analogies were widely used, as in the tradition's belief that Saint Patrick used the small shamrock plant to show how God could be both three and one. The Celtic Christian movement especially relied on poetry to engage the people's imaginations. One ancient poem, attributed to Saint David, exclaims,

> No man is the son of knowledge if he is not also the son of poetry.

No man loves poetry without loving the light,
Nor the light without loving the truth,
Nor the truth without loving justice,
Nor justice without loving God.[41]

The Celtic communication of Christian truth was known to combine genres, such as analogy and poetry, as in this early Irish verse:

Three folds of the cloth, yet only one napkin is there,
Three joints in the finger, but still only one finger fair;
Three leaves of the shamrock, yet no more than one shamrock to wear,
Frost, snow-flakes and ice, all in water their origin share,
Three Persons in God; to one God alone we make prayer.[42]

Celtic Christian advocates especially engaged barbarian imaginations through storytelling and poetry. The several Celtic peoples revered their oral traditions; their bards told stories and their poets recited poems that communicated the people's beliefs, history, and folk wisdom through entertainment. Their "poets constituted the intellectual aristocracy of Celtic society. . . . The Celts regarded poets as . . . intermediaries between this world and the next," and their storytelling bards were also greatly esteemed. "To a considerable extent, . . . Christian monks and scholars took over the role of the old Druidic bards and filid."[43] Many of them became prodigious storytellers. They communicated much of the biblical message by telling its stories, and many of their more original stories, and the stories of the saints, were passed to many generations through the oral tradition.

Celtic music is enormously popular once again, so we are not surprised to learn that Christianity engaged the Celtic peoples and other barbarians through music. The Celtic peoples were as musically oriented as any people of history. Ian Bradley reports, "The Celts sang as they worked, as they played and as they prayed."[44] Celtic music's distinctive repetitive and rhythmic qualities proved useful to the Christian revelation and to the development of devout souls and communities.

Vincent Donovan, the modern Catholic apostle to the Masai people of East Africa, once observed that Protestant Christian leaders seem to trust only the sense of hearing and therefore rely almost totally upon using the preached and taught Word to reach and teach people. By contrast, he said, Celtic Catholics have always known that God can use all five senses to "speak" to people.

Celtic Christians strongly illustrated this through their use of the visual arts. For instance, they used the famous Celtic knot, whose spirals intertwine endlessly to symbolize God's encircling protection of his people, to symbolize eternity, and to suggest the movement, pilgrimage, and progress that are essential in the Christian's life.[45] Celtic Christianity's distinctive tall standing cross, with a circle intersecting the upper half of the cross, was an imaginative way to visually integrate the themes of creation and redemption.[46] The biblical scenes sometimes carved at the base of a cross served as teaching aids.

The theme of imagination thus helps us see that Celtic Christians took an intentionally redundant approach to communicating Christianity. It never occurred to them to rely, as some traditions come close to, upon preaching alone to communicate the fullness of Christianity. They seem to have employed as many different media as they could to get the message across, in as many ways as possible, and to get people involved with the message and its expression.

As we have already seen, Kierkegaard anticipated Hammerback's second persona when he wrote that one way to achieve identification with a people is to stress possibility—that is, what the people's lives can become. Helping the

Irish to imagine what they could become may have been Patrick's most profound rhetorical achievement, all the more notable when we contrast Patrick with his near contemporary, Augustine. Thomas Cahill suggests:

> Patrick's emotional grasp of Christian truth may have been greater than Augustine's. Augustine looked into his own heart and found there the inexpressible anguish of each individual, which enabled him to articulate a theory of sin that has no equal—the dark side of Christianity. Patrick prayed, made peace with God, and then looked not only into his own heart but into the hearts of others. What he saw convinced him of the bright side—that even slave traders can turn into liberators, even murderers can act as peacemakers, even barbarians can take their place among the nobility of heaven.[47]

CHAPTER 6

The Missionary Perspective of Celtic Christianity

A t one level, the Celtic Christian leaders and people were a simple study. Their lives and communities were open books. In stark contrast to the secretive religion of the Druids, in which membership was restrictive and the priests never showed most of the cards in their hands, the monastic communities and the churches were open to everyone, with no secrets from anyone. They never claimed to be other than they were or more than they were. They were devoted, compassionate, sold-out citizens of heaven. They relied, through "prayer without ceasing," upon the triune God's providence and power. They would do anything they could to help other people find The Way.

At another level, however, the Celtic Christian movement functioned with such intuitive sophistication that, in the academic field of missiology, we have only recently learned enough to name and describe some of what they knew and did that contributed to their reach and expansion.

We have already explored some of these themes. We saw that the contagion of their movement was partly attributable to the formation of their people, in the monastic communities, for ministry and witness. We observed their apostolic band approach to planting churches in settlements and how their faith focused on people's middle daily issues as well as the ultimate religious issues. We saw how their ethos, their identification with the people, their emotional appeal, their imaginal appeal, and their call to a new identity all helped communicate the gospel. We saw how their strategy of indigenizing the forms for expressing Christianity in the life and culture of each "barbarian" population helped the gospel's meaning to break through time and again. By the eleventh century their culturally relevant movement had adapted Christianity to the language and culture of many different Celtic and Germanic peoples; indeed, the number of cultural adaptations that the movement managed was unprecedented.

We saw that they consistently paid the price to understand the target language and culture, although there were exceptions. Columba, we think, never really learned a Pictish language, so his occasional missions in Scotland employed an interpreter.[1] That is why we think he personally did more evangelism in his first career in Ireland than after he left for Iona "to convert the Picts." Nevertheless, he was a marvelous mission executive in Scotland, and his missionaries communicated through a Pictish culture and language.

We have not yet reflected upon the way in which, as part of their indigenization strategy, the pioneers of Celtic Christianity contextualized Christianity's message for the several Celtic peoples. The biblical revelation was primary, but understanding the people's cultural and historical context helped them to know what in Scripture to feature first, and how to "translate" it for the people. This principle is crucial because, as David Bosch observed, "the Christian faith never exists except as 'translated' into a culture."[2]

We can see the importance of the indigenization (or translation) principle through what may be a negative example in the history of the evangelization of Scotland's Picts. Most historians, following Bede, emphasize that Saint Columba's people evangelized the Picts of northern Scotland; it was not necessary to reach the Picts of southern Scotland because, they say, "Saint Ninian" had already reached them. We know very little about Ninian; most of what we do know comes from these lines in Bede's *Ecclesiastical History*:

> [Columba] came into Britain . . . to preach the word of God to the provinces of the northern Picts, who are separated from the southern parts by steep and rugged mountains; for the southern Picts, who dwell on this side of those mountains, had long before, as is reported, forsaken the errors of idolatry, and embraced the truth, by the preaching of Ninia[n], a most reverend bishop and holy man of the British nation, who had been regularly instructed at Rome, in the faith and mysteries of the truth; whose episcopal see, named after St. Martin the bishop, and famous for a stately church . . . is generally called the White House, because he there built a church of stone, which was not usual among the Britons.[3]

In a departure from his usual attention to detail, Bede tells us nothing about how Ninian and his people went about their mission, nor does he give dates for Ninian's ministry. Nora Chadwick reports that the traditional date for Ninian's founding of Whithorn is A.D. 397 and that he died around A.D. 432,[4] which would place his work in the early fifth century.

Now, one early source indicates that Ninian's work among the southern Picts did not endure. By the time Patrick wrote his "Letter against the Soldiers of Coroticus" (perhaps in the mid-450s), he refers twice to the southern Picts as "apostate," that is, no longer faithful to the Christian religion.[5] This is not, for Patrick, a mere rumor or an incidental allusion but a centerpiece in his antislavery drama; Coroticus's Briton soldiers have sold Patrick's Irish converts to the "vilest, worthless, apostate Picts."[6] Louis Gougaud also concluded that "the Southern Picts converted by Ninian did not persevere in the faith"; Columba's people, he suggests, had to reach the southern Picts again, as well as reach the northern Picts for the first time.[7]

We lack adequate knowledge of who Ninian and his people really reached from their base at Whithorn. Indeed, Hume Brown suggests that "who these Picts were and what is implied in this vague notion of their conversion will probably never be determined; and, as a matter of fact, all traces of Ninian's labours disappear during the centuries that followed the withdrawal of the [Roman] legion."[8]

The slender evidence suggests two possibilities. First, Ninian's mission may have confined its outreach to the southern Picts who had adopted the Latin language and Roman culture during the Roman occupation. Second, they may have reached Picts who had not been substantially Romanized except with culturally Roman Christianity.

In either case, the churches that Ninian's mission planted were small, in part because they marched to the Roman drum. At the Whithorn headquarters, the church was built out of stone (as the Romans would do) rather than from the planks and wattle that were used in culturally Celtic architecture. Bede, of course, enthusiastically sponsored Ninian's curriculum vitae because Ninian "had received orthodox instruction at Rome in the faith and the mysteries of the truth." We already know what that meant for the Roman wing of the Church and for Bede. It meant, as David Bosch reminds us, "that a 'missionary church' must reflect in every detail the Roman custom of the moment."[9] Ninian's mission underachieved because it imported Roman language and ways into a very different culture. The cemeteries that have survived are all Roman.

Why did the southern Picts fall away? It is possible that the first generation of southern Pict Christians understood the Christian message and ethic and became real Christians but a later generation lapsed into nominal faith or into paganism. That has happened in many other young churches in Christianity's history; indeed, every church struggles with the challenge of passing on the meaning of the faith to each succeeding generation. If Ninian planted small churches, and only in Romanized Pict communities, the movement would have lacked the critical mass necessary for long-term survival; and when the Romans went home, the churches lost their colonial support.

However, if Ninian did reach non-Romanized Picts with Roman Christianity, apparently they never really understood the Christianity they received from Ninian and his people—as presented in Latin language and Roman forms. More likely, however, the southern Picts understood enough from Roman Christianity to know, say, that they wanted to go to heaven, and they learned the Roman rituals enough to go through the motions—but without understanding enough Christian meaning to pass it on, in their own ways, to their children. That has happened in many other cases of mission, both Roman Catholic and Protestant; when the missionaries imposed Western forms, the people learned the foreign forms, but they could not sufficiently understand the meaning. As Bosch reminds us, "The Christian faith never [viably] exists except as 'translated' into a culture!"

In contrast to Ninian and Bede and the whole Roman wing of the Church, Celtic Christian leaders understood the indigenizing principle and the need for the principle, and they developed some sophistication in selectively applying the principle. For example, they understood that the Christian movement should always employ the people's language. They probably observed that using indigenous music is usually most effective, but some "foreign" music will catch on, and some music of the whole Church will enrich their identity. In the communication of Christianity's essential message, they undoubtedly discovered that many of the transcultural teachings and stories of the Scriptures were easily communicated in the tribal cultures of Britain and Europe, but additional contextualization is always useful. Three examples will demonstrate this insight.

The first example focuses on the doctrine of the Trinity and demonstrates that, in the specific sociocultural context, some opportunities to contextualize will be rather obvious to any Christian communicator who studies the target culture.

Patrick would have observed several traits in the Irish Celts that, together, suggested one communicative response. The Irish, perhaps from the teachings of the Druids or the primal religion that preceded the Druids, were aware that Ultimate Reality was mysterious and complex, and they were comfortable with paradox; nevertheless, they had "a bureaucrat's love of classification."[10] Brendan Lehane reports that the Irish also believed that some numbers were significant; they found the number three especially fascinating, and their characteristic way of structuring thought about complex matters was

> the triad, an arrangement of three statements which summed up a thing or person or quality or mood, or simply linked otherwise incompatible things. Three false sisters were said to be "perhaps," "maybe" and "I dare say": three timid brothers "Hush," "Stop," and "Listen." The three keys that unlock thoughts were drunkenness, trustfulness, love. . . . If there were paradox or pun in a triad, so much the better. . . . The Irish had their liking for riddles too. . . . Everyone was thought to be spiritually tied to three . . . lumps of earth, the three sods of fate. The first was that on which he was born, the sod of birth. Second was that on which he died. And the third marked the place of his burial.[11]

The Irish Celts even imagined some of their gods and (especially) goddesses in groups of threes, and one god was believed to have three faces! Now, given such knowledge of the people, most missionaries would readily perceive that the Irish people had been shaped by history, by culture, and by preparatory grace to appreciate a trinitarian explanation of the High God. So, when Irish seekers asked Patrick how Christianity understood God, his response drew from the doctrine of the Trinity:

> Our God is the God of all people, the God of heaven and earth. . . . His life is in all things; he makes all things live; he governs all things; he supports all things. . . . He has a son who is coeternal with him and of like nature . . . and the Holy Spirit breathes in them. The Father, the Son and the Holy Spirit are not separate.[12]

The doctrine of the Trinity became the foundational paradigm for Celtic Christianity. The doctrine informed the people's piety as well as the theologians' theories. Furthermore, the understanding of God as a unity of three persons, bound together in love, informed the Celtic model for life in Christian community; the understanding of God as a family of three persons defined the Christian family. Celtic Christians lived their daily lives, from waking up to cleaning up, from working to retiring, aware of the presence, protection, and guidance of all three persons of the Trinity.

Their understanding of the doctrine was like the Roman understanding, with two exceptions: First, the Romans, more than the Celts, emphasized the oneness, or unity, of the Trinity. Second, the Roman Christians emphasized the transcendence of the triune God (later expressed visibly in their Gothic cathedrals); God was rather distant, if not remote, except for Christ's real presence in the sacraments and access to him through the saints. The Celtic Christians, however, emphasized the immanence of the triune God as Companion in this life and the next; in their experience, the veil between earth and heaven was thin—*if* you viewed creation as sacramental. Many centuries after Patrick and

Columba, Celtic Christians in the Hebrides Islands prepared for evening prayer with this affirmation:

I lie down this night with God,
    And God will lie down with me;
I lie down this night with Christ,
    And Christ will lie down with me;
I lie down this night with the Spirit,
    And the Spirit will lie down with me;
God and Christ and the Spirit
    Be lying down with me.[13]

The second example of Celtic indigenization focuses on a contextually appropriate way to interpret the death of Christ. Thomas Cahill tells us that the Irish were still practicing human sacrifice when Patrick returned. They sacrificed some prisoners of war to appease the war gods, some of their own newborns to appease the harvest gods, and occasionally a prince would offer himself as a sacrifice to some deity whose help was needed.

Three principles drove this sacrificial tradition. First, there were always devoted religious people who were willing to give up their lives to the gods for the people. Second, there were always "basely religious"[14] people who were willing to sacrifice other people to the gods! Third, "it would be an understatement to assert that the Irish gods were not the friendliest of figures."[15] Their gods were capricious; they prepared traps for people; and they blessed people only in response to flattery, liturgical manipulation, and sacrifice. That religious worldview produced a precarious sense of life; probably every Irishman was familiar with the experience of cosmic terror.

Patrick proclaimed the good news of a different kind of God. Christianity's God is not hostile, capricious, or self-seeking; he is for us, he loves people (and his other creatures), and he wills their deliverance from sin and terror into new life. Patrick, drawing from the Philippian Hymn, proclaimed that this God does not want people to feed him through human sacrifices; this God has sacrificed his only Son for us and wants to feed us through the blessed sacrament. No human being needs to be sacrificed ever again. This High God calls us not to die for him, but to live for him and for one another.[16]

The third example also focuses on a contextualized way to interpret the death of Jesus, developed by Saint Aidan as he came to understand the history and values of the Anglo-Saxons of northern England. In A.D. 625, eight years before Iona commissioned Aidan to Northumbria, Canterbury had commissioned Paulinus to the same region. Paulinus, in the tradition of Ninian, must have imported left-brained, culturally Roman Christianity. Bede's account begins by asserting that "The nation of the Northumbrians . . . received the faith through the preaching of Paulinus."[17] Bede soon admits, however, that the "heathen" were unresponsive to Paulinus's preaching, and indeed Paulinus "labored much . . . to retain those that went with him, by the help of God, that they should not revolt from the faith."[18] Paulinus did make some progress with King Edwin and his associates, though the king did not immediately accept the faith.

One day a neighboring king sent a messenger to Edwin's court. Inside his scroll was a poisoned dagger. As the messenger charged to stab Edwin, one member of the court, Lilla, was close enough to step across and take the dagger in his own stomach. The dagger passed through Lilla's body and also wounded Edwin, though not fatally. That night Edwin's queen gave birth to a daughter. Following these two experiences, Edwin asked Paulinus to baptize his baby daughter and eleven other members of his household. In time, after more teaching and reflection (and an inviting letter from the pope), "King Edwin, therefore, with all the nobility of the nation, and a large number of the common sort, received the faith, and the washing of regeneration in . . . 627"[19]

In time, King Edwin was slain, and Paulinus moved on to serve the church at Rochester. One gets the impression, reading Bede's sections on Aidan's ministry from Lindisfarne, that Aidan and his people found the number of common people who were already converts, or even pre-evangelized, to be much less "vast" than Bede's earlier hype of Paulinus's work had suggested.

Nevertheless, Aidan built upon something important from that history. People told him the story of Lilla, King Edwin's associate, who had taken the poisoned dagger intended for the king. Aidan perceived that the courage, loyalty, and devotion that were embodied in Lilla's deed represented ultimate values in this people's culture. Indeed, the deed steeled their conviction that there would be no greater honor than to die for the king they served.

David Adam reports Aidan's rhetorical response. Aidan told them that he and his people also served as the "soldiers" of a King—for whom they were willing to risk wild animals, hostile armies, or even death until this whole world becomes the Kingdom of their King.

Then Aidan added the punch line. He and other Christian soldiers had come to represent the King who loved his soldiers and people so much that the King laid down his life for them! In dying, the King won a kingdom for his followers.

So Christians have a supreme purpose for living in this world, to serve Christ and to live for the glory of God in doing his will. They also have a definite reward. Soldiers on earth can be rewarded only if the king is the victor. Life can be eternal, and people can be set free, because Christ has won the victory.[20]

Sometimes the mission context serves not only as a theater for adapting the presentation of Christianity to the people; the context can serve also as a catalyst for recovering something essential and precious within Christianity from the people.[21] For instance, the Celtic Christian approach to nature was a very distinctive feature of Celtic Christianity and also represented an important Christian rediscovery—from the barbarians! One day, as Patrick and several companions were surveying the land at Armagh where a church would be built,

> they climbed to that hilltop—and they came on a doe with its little fawn lying in the place where is now the northern altar of the church in Armagh. Patrick's companions wished to catch the fawn and kill it; but Patrick refused to permit this; instead he caught the fawn himself and carried it on his shoulders, and the doe followed him like a gentle loving sheep until he released the fawn on another hillside to the north of Armagh.[22]

The story of Patrick and the deer is one of many such stories. Virtually every Celtic saint was noted for his or her great fondness of, and rapport with, animals and birds. Columba's Iona served as a sanctuary for migratory birds and a hospital for injured birds; his legend tells of a favored horse shedding tears as Columba lay dying. Two otters befriended Cuthbert as he prayed while standing in the sea. Columbanus had squirrels, wolves, and other wild animals among his friends. The tradition around Saint Kevin of Glendalough tells us that a badger brought him a daily salmon to eat, that birds surrounded him in song as he prayed, and that he once experienced a blackbird laying an egg in his open hand as he prayed. Michael Mitton suggests that "the very strong presence of the Spirit of God in such people affected the animals' response to them."[23]

Somewhat later, the life of Francis of Assisi would feature similar stories of rapport with nature's creatures, which was also interpreted as a sign of the Holy Spirit within him. Such love for animals was extraordinary in the Roman wing of the Church; it was comparatively ordinary in the Celtic wing. Indeed, scholars surmise that Francis probably "caught" the Celtic Christian love for nature in his visits to Bobbio, the Celtic monastic community near Assisi.

The Roman Church has always celebrated the life of Francis, but the fact that it regards his love for nature's creatures as extraordinary indicates Roman Christianity's more detached or impersonal approach to nature.[24] We can observe the difference in their preferred settings for worship: the Celts loved to celebrate the gospel in the open air; the Roman branch preferred thick buildings that walled out the sights and sounds from the world. Roman Christianity's detachment from nature, in time, opened the way for Western humanity's later domination and exploitation of nature—which Celtic Christians would have regarded as sinful.

How do we account for Celtic Christianity's reverence for nature's creatures? Ian Bradley suggests that the Celtic love for nature sprang from three "roots."[25] First, love for God's creation is biblical. Genesis declares the goodness and preciousness of God's creation; the Psalms are filled with a sense of creation's wonder; and Jesus taught that the birds and animals, and even the plants, matter to God. Second, from the Druids' nature-mysticism that preceded Christianity's arrival, the pagan Celts already respected and revered nature; the Christianity that Patrick brought affirmed and Christianized their affinity with nature. Third, Celtic Christians lived in natural settings, so their experience informed their love of nature.

To be sure, the Celts' orientation toward nature changed with their Christianization. On the one hand, Christian faith enhanced the Celts' love for nature while also arming them with God's providence as they faced nature's threats. On the other hand, it changed the way they viewed nature as a source for knowing the Divine. They moved from pantheism, gods in nature, to a Christian panentheism: the transcendent God, who is revealed in the history of Israel and in Christ, can also be known through nature. They now knew that the history recorded in Scripture was God's primary mode of revelation; nature was now the "second book of God."[26]

This point is not easy to communicate, but I recall the memorable way that Ted Runyon of Emory University's Candler School of Theology once clarified it: "The psalmist did not say, 'The heavens declare the glory of God and the firmament shows his handiwork.' The psalmist was declaring that the heavens declare the glory of Yahweh and the firmament shows his handiwork." Celtic Christianity believed that the natural world was created good, and although the Fall introduced sin and evil into the natural order, it was still essentially God's good creation. Celtic Christians also believed that the veil between the natural and the supernatural, and between earth and heaven, was much thinner—especially at holy places—than the Roman wing believed. Consequently, nature figures prominently in their visual Christian symbols.

Ian Bradley observes:

> The artwork which the Celts have left us as their most tangible legacy is full of the exuberant celebration of creation. The borders of the illustrations in their illuminated manuscripts are often made up of intertwining patterns of fruit and foliage. Beautifully executed drawings of birds and animals serve as punctuation marks on the pages of script. The distinctive feature of the Celtic Cross is the circle of creation, representing the earth and the sun, which surrounds and encompasses the cross of redemption.[27]

The Celtic Christians' attitude toward nature could teach us several things today. First, their affirmation of nature stands as an outstanding example of a Christian mission moving into a culture and affirming, and building upon, what it can. Second, they model the fact that a missionary encounter with another culture can often help us perceive, and recover, something precious in the Christian body of truth. Third, because they understood nature so intimately that they saw both the wonder and the threat, they would dissuade us from the naive New Age romanticism about nature often expressed today. Fourth, they would say that our lives can be deeply enriched by living in covenant with creation as well as Creator; the birds and animals can bless us. Fifth, they would remind us of the basic biblical mandate for God's people to be the stewards of creation, that our exploitation of creation has polluted the earth and introduced an undeniable ecological crisis, so they would counsel us to abandon our denial and commit to loving and restoring the Lord's good earth.

I experience the most dissonance, even discomfort, in considering the Celtic Christian doctrine of human nature. Celtic Christianity's belief in the goodness of creation—infected (but not destroyed) by sin and evil—was matched by a belief in an essential goodness of human nature, to which you could appeal in evangelism.

It is important to acknowledge the roots of Celtic Christianity's optimism about human nature. Genesis sees people created in God's image, and Psalm 8 can still affirm that humans are only a little lower than the angels and are crowned with glory and honor. The Druids (apparently) had believed in free will and the possibility of willing to live a good life—and succeeding. The Greek fathers of the Eastern church had believed that sin had not obliterated the image of God in people or destroyed their capacity to want, and enjoy, fellowship with God. Origen in Egypt and Irenaeus in Gall held similar views. From these influences, and from their reflections from Scripture and mission experience, Ian Bradley tells us that Celtic Christianity viewed "human nature not as being radically tainted by sin and evil, intrinsically corrupt and degenerate, but as imprinted with the image of God, full of potential and opportunity, longing for completion and perfection."[28]

The Roman Church, however, especially under the sway of Saint Augustine, had a significantly different view of human nature. Augustine, arguably Christianity's greatest and most profound theological giant, had reflected his way into the view that original sin had so corrupted human nature, and twisted it into such pride and selfishness, that people were no longer free to will what God wills. Consequently, everything involved in the salvation of people is by the grace of the sovereign God; people do not have enough goodness left within them to even cooperate in their salvation or, once saved, to live a good life without more grace.

Augustine's high doctrine of grace, which even suggested that grace is irresistible, and coupled with his observation that some people do in fact resist grace, seems to have led him to a logical conclusion later expanded by John Calvin: double election. God, apparently, has "wired" some people to be receptive to God's grace, but not other people. This difference between Roman and Celtic Christianity is very important for evangelization because the two views lead to quite contrasting understandings of what is essentially involved in salvation. For Augustine, Jesus Christ saves us by rescuing us from sin and the consequences of the Fall. For the Celtic apostles, Jesus Christ comes to restore our humanity and to complete his good creation.[29]

While I do not pretend to occupy an Olympian vantage point from which I can presume to settle the most enduring problem in a theology of human nature, I believe that several observations are warranted. First, Celtic Christianity's theological optimism about human nature cannot adequately account for the Holocaust and the many other cases of genocide and man's inhumanity to man. Augustine's doctrine of human nature does more adequately account for large-scale depravity and for much else that has gone terribly wrong in God's human experiment. Second, it is possible to observe, in most people, both sin and goodness. Third, my interviews with converts indicate that, for many people, becoming a Christian involves experiences of being rescued and experiences of being completed. Fourth, the Celtic Christian movement suggests that it is often more effective to begin with people at the point of their goodness, however latent, than to initially engage people as sinners. Fifth, the Celtic doctrine of human nature enabled Celtic Christians to perceive God's possibilities in the "barbarians," and they engaged in mission to these peoples for five centuries. The Roman doctrine, combined with their expectation that a people be sufficiently civilized to be reachable, energized much less mission in these same centuries.

The Celtic missionaries, in every case, reached out to a tribe of people who were already influenced by, perhaps devoted to, one or more religious traditions. These were "primal" or "folk" religions; the best known of these religions today is the religion of the Druids.[30] Every missionary today, indeed every Christian who is engaged in the ministry of witness today, engages people who already have a worldview and are already influenced by, and see the world through and may be devoted to, one or more religions or philosophies.

The basic ways that the Celtic Christian movement engaged people who already had a religion can instruct us today. On one occasion, in "the territory of Corcu Temne," Patrick came to "the well of Findmag." Tirechan reports, "[D]ruids honoured the well and made votive offerings in it as if to a god." Once, a seer had provided that his bones would be placed under the rock in the well, so "for this reason they worshipped the well as a god." Patrick, with the help of "my God who lives in heaven," lifted the stone. "They found nothing in the well but water alone, and they believed in the high God."[31] Beside the stone, Patrick baptized a man named Cata.

The Celtic Christian leaders were radical trinitarian monotheists who, therefore, saw no reason to welcome other gods into the life of Christian communities. Occasionally, they would confront the local god of their leaders—as in Patrick's occasional "power encounter" with the Druids, or as in the case where Columbanus had to "cleanse" an area by chopping down sacred trees that had become idols.

Such encounters, however, were extraordinary. Michael Mitton observes that Celtic Christian leaders relied strongly on the "spiritual gift of discernment," so they "were very sensitive to presences of good and evil in people and places. They therefore sensed what was good in a community and blessed it accordingly, or they sensed evil, in which case they sought to combat it with prayer."[32] The power encounters were infrequent, however, and the settings requiring a "slash and burn" approach were even less frequent. Furthermore, "nowhere do you get the impression of a powerful ecclesiastical force moving in on reluctant individuals."[33]

Generally, a mission team would visit a Celtic settlement, befriend the people, and engage in conversation and some presentation to "make known God's gift and the eternal comfort He provides."[34] In time, they would invite the people to confess faith and form into a church, but there was no manipulation, coercion, or force; they believed Christ wanted people's free response. They studied the host culture and affirmed and built on every indigenous feature that they could. They affirmed, for instance, the Celtic people's religious aspirations, their sense of divinity's closeness, their belief in an afterlife, their love for creation, and as we have seen, their fascination with the number three. Celtic missionaries seem to have believed that God's prevenient grace had preceded them and prepared the people for the gospel. They seem to have believed that, just as Jesus came to the Jews not to destroy the law and the prophets but to fulfill them, so he comes to every people "not to destroy, but to fulfill" their religious tradition.

We can see this policy visually in the evolution of the tall Celtic stone crosses. When Patrick returned to Ireland, the Irish Celts already worshiped around tall "standing stones." The pillars stood as a symbol of the people's desire to reach up to the heavens and the High God; they stood as a symbolic link between heaven and earth. Once, when the people were more nomadic, a tall tree might serve as such a symbol; when they gathered into settlements, the standing stone became the favored symbol.[35] When a people turned to the Christian faith, the people often Christianized their standing stone by carving or painting a cross, the sign of the fish, or the Chi-Rho symbol on the stone, and it became a place made sacred for Christian worship. In time, this practice led to the sculpting, from tall stones, of tall standing Celtic crosses with the circle intersecting the cross. In time, biblical scenes and/or nature scenes were carved onto some crosses.

The Celtic Christian movement often built chapels on or near the grove, the well, or the hill that had served as a sacred site for the primal religion. The sacred site would often retain its former name or a reminiscent name. Celtic Christianity often retained and Christianized some of the prior religion's holy days, festivals, and ceremonies, thereby grafting the new onto the old. Christian priests and monks often wore a clothing or hairstyle reminiscent of the people's former priests. Celtic Christianity preferred continuity rather than discontinuity, inclusion rather than exclusion. Celtic Christianity was a fairly religion-friendly movement.

Celtic Christianity's religion-friendly policy would not have been very controversial in the early Middle Ages; indeed, the Roman wing's mission practice sometimes followed a similar policy. This is most memorably noted in the letter, which Bede has preserved for posterity, that Pope Gregory once sent to his missionaries at Canterbury:

I have, upon mature deliberation on the affair of the English, determined . . . that the temples of the idols in that nation ought not to be destroyed; but let the idols that are in them be destroyed; let holy water be made and sprinkled in the said temples, let altars be erected, and relics placed. For if those temples are well built, it is requisite that they be converted from the worship of devils to the service of the true God; that the nation, seeing that their temples are not destroyed, may remove error from their hearts, and know and adore the true God.[36]

Gregory also directed a missiological response to the Angle practice of slaughtering cattle as sacrifices to devils: "No more [let them] offer beasts to the Devil, but kill cattle to the praise of God in their eating, and return thanks to the Giver of all things for their sustenance."[37]

So, the Roman wing of the Church may, at least by the seventh century, have had no serious problem with the Celtic movement's religion-friendly policy. We have seen, however, that the Roman wing of the Church had serious problems with the Celts' culture-friendly policy.

CHAPTER 7

The Relevance of First-Millennium Celtic Christianity for Third-Millennium Western Christianity

With the exception of events reported in Scripture, most church leaders seem to assume that something that happened more than a thousand years ago could not possibly be relevant to the world we now live in and the challenges we face today. This assumption, of course, is understandable. The social worlds of Ireland and western Europe, in the second half of Christianity's first millennium, were astonishingly different from our Western setting in the early third millennium. Even *early* modern innovations like Gutenberg's printing press and Galileo's telescope, the Pony Express and Morse code, and sulfa drugs, wireless radio, and "heavier-than-air flight" would not surface in history for many hundreds of years. When Bede wrote his *Ecclesiastical History* in A.D. 731 the people never watched the evening news or surfed the Internet; they did not text (or tweet) each other; they did not blow-dry their hair. Most of the people never saw a city approaching the size of today's Sioux Falls, South Dakota.

Since the relevance of this ancient movement is not widely assumed, most church leaders perceive the Church's first millennium issues as quaint, even interesting, but irrelevant. Let me suggest, however, that beneath the many obvious differences between their time and ours, some similarities also lurk; at the level of principles, some of their issues are among our issues too.

Take, for instance, their issue of the "right" date for celebrating Easter. At the surface level the issue now seems comparatively trivial, but the deeper issue of *conformity* is still much with us. The churches in most denominations and networks are expected to comply with certain customs and with the directives from headquarters or from some leader or leader-group; the penalties for not complying vary from one tradition to another, but consequences follow.

Again, when we read that the Roman wing of the Church essentially withheld outreach to people who did not speak the Latin *language*, the policy now seems laughable, and the Celtic multilingual strategy seems like a no-brainer. However, most of the churches I work with essentially withhold outreach from people who do not speak English. In my part of the world, at the assumption level, English is about as entrenched today as Latin was in eighth-century Europe. The people in the city in which I live, Lexington, Kentucky, speak at least thirty-five languages in their homes, but most of Lexington's churches wait for English to become the people's first language before inviting them. The country in which I live, the United States, has become the most multilingual nation-state on earth, and the most multilingual nation-state in human history. In the United States, however, most of the churches do church in English only, and most of the churches that declare inclusiveness as their top value do church in English only. Old paradigms change their appearance, but they resist serious change.

Other parallels come to mind. The Roman wing of the Church regarded *literacy* as a prerequisite to people's Christianization. Today, although that is no church's official policy, many preliterate or semiliterate people inhabit our communities, but evangelical churches seldom invite people who are not confident readers to participatory Bible studies, and Episcopal churches seldom invite people who cannot navigate the *Book of Common Prayer*. (Pentecostal churches, however, often engage preliterate people.)

Again, the ancient Roman Church's de facto policy that people who were not culturally Roman were "barbarian" and, therefore, were unfit for Christianization seems ludicrous when viewed through history's rearview mirror. Most churches today, however, expect pre-Christian people to be *like church people* culturally; they are expected to understand and speak the church's accent and vocabulary, to share the church's aesthetic preferences, to dress and look like church people, to vote like church people, to live their lives in ways that church people can approve, and so on. If they are not already "like us," they may never be invited by any church.

Overall, Roman-like exclusionary attitudes and practices are more epidemic in churches today than almost anyone recognizes. A church may *say*, "We are a friendly church," "Inclusiveness is our priority," or "Everyone is welcome," but most people only visit a church, or join a church, *if* the church invites them; and there are many types of people that the most "inclusive" churches never really invite and make room for. We can say of most churches that Laotian-speaking people; preliterate people; addictive people; cohabiting people; bikers; divorced people; ex-prisoners; people with "reputations"; people with anger issues; people who "are not nice"; pedophiles; people who are blind, deaf, mentally disabled, or mentally ill; post–high school youth; couples without children; single mature men; single mature women; celebrities; wealthy people; famous people; people in power positions; and *many* others need not apply.

If I may speak autobiographically, I have observed and experienced the range of a church's possible policies for lost people. When I experienced a spiritual awakening as a teenager in south Florida, I started visiting churches.

Several of the churches in our community were not interested in me; my reputation had preceded me! But the Fulford Methodist Church welcomed me to my true home, and I became a Christ-follower there.

Seven years later, while in divinity school, I was doing pastoral visits in a Florida hospital and befriended a young nurse who shared that she was divorced, with a child. I was to speak that Sunday evening at the Methodist church near her home, so I invited her to visit. At the reception after the service, the pastor was unwilling to meet her.

Decades later, also in Florida, I discovered a contrasting policy. First Baptist Church of Leesburg had grown, in twenty years, from 400 to 7,200 members. The church started growing when the leaders decided to "spend our lives befriending and inviting all the people we can find that no other church seems to want."[1]

So, the issues that the Celtic Christian leaders faced and substantially resolved, and the approaches in ministry and mission that they pioneered, *might* be more relevant to Western Christianity today than we have usually perceived. One feature of Celtic Christianity has already demonstrated great relevance and experienced a renaissance: Celtic spirituality.

Many church leaders have discovered an interest in Celtic spirituality because the spiritual formation crisis in the majority of active church members has become undeniable. Our denominations are, today, underachievers. My own denomination, The United Methodist Church, once started one or two new churches per day; today, we start three or four a month. Once we supported more than 2,500 foreign missionaries; today we support less than 400. Once we received more than 400,000 new Christians per year; today we receive less than 200,000.

These trends, undoubtedly, have multiple causes, but one cause is the thin faith of 80 percent of the country's church attendees. As Garrison Keillor observes: "Most people do not really believe. They have tried to believe and they wish they did believe and are sorry that they don't, because they like to be around people who do. So they come to church and enjoy the music and hallowedness of it all, but the faith is not in them."[2]

The situation is even more complicated than Keillor knows. The faith that is in many church attendees is as much American folk religion as Christianity. Their focus tends to be *consumerist* ("What's in it for me?"), *moralistic* ("Live by the rules!"), *therapeutic* ("I want peace of mind and happiness") *Deism*. As I overhear God's people talk, Christianity is almost reduced to accepting Christ as your Savior so you can go to heaven when you die, and between now and then you attend church, have a daily devotional, live a clean life, and "let" God meet your needs and attain your goals.[3] There may be more right than wrong in that reduction of the faith, but it is a form of Christianity with some of the heart removed, more of the mind, and most of the vertebrae. It is not a version of the Christian faith that has a fair chance of changing the world or its devotees. No ancient martyrs would have been fed to the lions if their faith had been reduced to that.

The problem of nominal syncretistic faith is not brand new. Kierkegaard perceived a version of the problem in nineteenth-century European state-church Christianity, and he challenged it in writings like *Attack upon "Christendom."* What is different today is that *many* church leaders have perceived that the piety occupying most pews produces the spiritual equivalent of scrub pines but not redwoods. Such faith lacks the deep roots that weather storms, that produce reproductive Christians who live in faith, hope, and love, who become saints engaging in ministry, working for peace and justice, and reaching lost people. So there is more interest today in the spiritual formation of the people of God than at any other time that anyone can remember, and many of these church leaders are gravitating toward Celtic spirituality.

The Celtic approach to the formation of Christians is, indeed, an enduring treasure; it is our "once and future" source. Alas, spiritual formation is not the focus of this book, but fortunately a wealth of literature is now available. Many people swear by three marvelous collections of writings—Oliver Davies's edited and compiled *Celtic Spirituality,* and the Northumbria Community's *Celtic Daily Prayer.* In *Holy Companions: Spiritual Practices from the Celtic Saints,* Mary Earle and Sylvia Maddox draw, chapter by chapter, from what can be known from a range of early medieval saints.

I have found interpretations like Esther de Waal's *Every Earthly Blessing: Rediscovering the Celtic Tradition* and Ray Simpson's *Exploring Celtic Spirituality: Historic Roots for Our Future* to be very useful. (One should be discriminating in acquiring books on Celtic spirituality; there are more books than most budgets can justify, and some writers are most interested in recovering the *pagan* spiritual practices that preceded Celtic Christianity's evangelization of Europe.) The following top ten perspectives, insights, and counsel from the Celtic Christian tradition, however, are underrepresented in the spirituality literature today, so I will briefly feature them:

1. Celtic Christian leaders would counsel today's church leaders to relinquish the full responsibility for making Christians into better Christians. Church leaders cannot do it *for* people—through preaching harder, scheduling more prayer meetings and retreats, or making all other attempts to do it *for* people through more and better programming. As we have already learned in the field of adult education, delegate to the people the *responsibility for their own development.* There are limits to what any leaders or

programs can achieve in the learning and lives of passive attendees; there are no known limits to what people can become through their own disciplines *and* (even more important) through nurturing one another's development.

2. They would counsel us to relinquish the illusion that Gutenberg's printing press produced a panacea. From the first printing of Bibles, in the 1450s, Protestant leaders seem to have assumed that if every church member had his or her own copy of the canon we would produce a biblically literate, rooted, informed church. It has never happened in more than five centuries. There is no reason to be confident that it will happen tomorrow—no matter how many translations and paraphrases are published, marketed, and promoted. Celtic Christian leaders would remind us that, before Gutenberg, Christians *memorized* much of the Bible. In the monastic communities, they came to know all 150 psalms, and much of the rest of the Bible, more or less by heart. The Scripture that is in us informs much more of our ongoing internal conversation than Scripture that we merely read.

3. They would counsel us to relinquish the illusion that a brief daily devotional each morning, in which (say) people read a snippet of Scripture, a brief reflection, and a short prayer—all on one page of *The Upper Room* devotional guide—will shape great souls. The people of Alcoholics Anonymous have learned to begin *and end* each day in devotional focus. The ancient Celtic practice scheduled three times per day, as modeled in Ray Simpson's *A Holy Island Prayer Book: Morning, Midday, and Evening Prayer* and in the Northumbria Community's *Celtic Daily Prayer*.

4. Not even three scheduled times for prayer each day make for powerful Christian spirituality. The most important practice, as the Celts recalled Paul's words,

is to "pray without ceasing" (1 Thessalonians 5:17). That is, you pray into each of the day's situations, events, responsibilities, and tasks, and you include the Holy Spirit in your ongoing internal conversation.

5. Feel free, often, to pray with your eyes wide open. Often, you *have* to keep your eyes open when you pray while driving, speaking, attending a meeting, or conversing with someone. But praying with one's eyes open is not a regretful necessity or a second-class approach. Closed is not necessarily better than open. The Celtic Christian saints often prayed with their eyes open, using something in the creation around them to fix on as a sign of God's presence.

6. Harness your *imagination* in your life of devotion to God. The saints imagined the Lord before them, behind them, above them, within them, or meeting them through a creature of the forest or a person in need. Imagination focuses and catalyzes prayer. (See Esther de Waal's *The Celtic Way of Prayer: The Recovery of the Religious Imagination*.)

7. They would recommend that every Christian have an *anam cara*—that is, a "soul friend." One's soul friend, as I understand it, is not a superior or even one's spiritual director, but a peer with whom one can be open and vulnerable. (John O'Donohue's *Anam Cara: A Book of Celtic Wisdom* takes the place of the single source that we never had before!)

8. Meet weekly or biweekly in a *small group* in which you are in ministry with one another, rejoicing and weeping with one another, pulling for one another, interceding for one another, holding one another accountable, bringing out the best in one another, identifying one another's gifts of the Spirit, and in which you learn to engage in ministry and to converse about the faith.

9. In your spiritual life, do *not* engage in endless ongoing self-assessment and spiritual navel-gazing. Canon Bryan Green, a great Anglican evangelist in the Celtic tradition, once said that too many Christians remind him of the fellow who planted a small bush in a pot and watered it every day—and pulled it out of the soil every day to see if the roots were growing! (Of course, they were not.) The purpose of the spiritual life, after all, is not to reinforce the pride, self-preoccupation, and narcissism that are our original sin, but to become open enough to the Spirit to be pulled out of that self-centeredness; to be reconciled to God, others, and creation; and to have the marvelous freedom of largely *forgetting oneself* for stretches of time—before regrouping in scheduled times of discipline.

10. The main purpose in the life of Christian devotion is not so much to get blessed, get our needs met, become happier, or accomplish any of the other early goals that people usually have in mind when they begin praying. The main purpose is to *become like Christ*. As C. S. Lewis reminded us, the Holy Spirit wants to make us "little Christs." Thomas á Kempis was right; it is about "the imitation of Christ." In life's ultimate paradox, as we become more like Christ—living by the will of God, reflecting the love of God—we become more like the people we were born to be and have really always wanted to be.

There are three more main purposes around the issue of formation that are so indispensable, and so supremely important, that they ought not be vulnerable to getting lost in a stack of ten points. I feature these points, especially, because many people with a new Celtic interest have bypassed them.

First, Celtic Christianity is *much* more than Celtic spirituality. As we have seen, it represents an alternative version of Christianity—involving some distinctive theological convictions, less individualism and more of life in community, understanding and adapting to the host culture, ministering to one another and reaching out to others through teams, "belonging before believing," and distinctive approaches to the faith's communication and to ministry, evangelism, mission, and much more. More important, compared to the Roman wing, Celtic Christianity was essentially a lay movement. Most important, the Church's Celtic wing lived by a contrasting conviction regarding Christianity's main business. Too many people who are into Celtic spirituality today have cherry-picked the ancient Celtic tradition—choosing one or two features they like while missing the Big Picture *and* the supremely important features.

Second, the formation of Christians is more than the *spiritual* formation of Christians. The people's formation in monastic community involved formation in theological knowledge, ministry skills, conversation skills, leadership, and more. Spiritual formation, by itself and no matter how well done, will not sufficiently renew the Church for its main business.

Third, our spiritual formation is not the ultimate goal; it is a *means* to achieving Christianity's main business. In the Celtic tradition, we do not immerse our minds in Scripture and pray virtually without ceasing that we might be blessed, but that we might bless others—within and beyond the Church. Our formation is for the sake of ministry and mission; most of our needs are met as we lose ourselves for the sake of Christ and his reign in human experience and human affairs. We are, incrementally and over time, formed in the likeness of Christ in order to be *liberated* from our self-interest and narcissism and, more important, to be given the credibility, the compassion, and the power from which ministry and mission make a difference.

As C. S. Lewis reminded us, "The church exists for nothing else but to draw men into Christ, to make them little Christs. If they are not doing that, all the cathedrals, clergy, missions, even the Bible itself, are simply a waste of time. God became man for no other purpose. It is even doubtful, you know, whether the whole universe was created for any other purpose."[4]

CHAPTER 8

The Celtic Future of the Christian Movement in the West

e have reflected on the Celtic Christianity that reached the Irish, the Picts, the Anglo-Saxons, and many other "barbarian" peoples; reached Europe a second time; brought Europe out of the Dark Ages and saved civilization; and then was pressured into conformity to Roman ways by the Church's politically dominant Roman wing. The story is a treasure within the total Christian story. As we acknowledged in chapter 7, however, the Celtic apostolic experiment may not seem very relevant to Western churches in the twenty-first century. After all, the Celtic project ended a thousand years ago and it engaged contexts very different from our age of cities, mass transportation, climate control, outer space, technology, and the Internet.

This book has addressed the issue of relevance especially at four points. The topic surfaces in the preface, and chapter 7 addressed related and recurring issues like conformity, language, literacy, and formation.

Chapter 1 concluded with the suggestion that, as in Patrick's time, establishment Christian leaders still take a dim view of pastors and churches who befriend pagans, sinners, and lost people, and who make apostolic outreach a church's priority. Establishment Christianity seems *always* to expect its people, pastors, and bishops to care for, and fraternize with, church people.

Chapter 3 concluded by suggesting that, as in the case of

the ancient Roman wing of the Church, denominations are still substantially in the hands of the less apostolic wing of the Church, which works overtime to gain and retain institutional control; which assumes it knows best; and which works persistently to impose Roman, European, or other culturally alien forms on the more indigenous and growing movements within the denomination. This pathology is observed today, for example, in most denominations in the United States that were "imported from Europe."

Three additional suggestions should establish the relevance of the Celtic Christian story to much of what Western Christianity faces in the twenty-first century.

First, a host of New Barbarians substantially populate the Western world once again; indeed, they are all around us. Many of them are secular—that is, they have never been substantially influenced by the Christian religion; they have no Christian memory; they have no church to return to.[1] Many have never acquired a "church etiquette" (they would not know when to stand, where to find 2 Corinthians, or what to say to the pastor after the service), and they have never experienced the kind of socialization to prepare them to fit and feel comfortable in a church. Often, they are thought to lack class. They may have unshined shoes or body odor or grease under their fingernails; in conversation, they might split an infinitive or utter an expletive. Many New Barbarians are addicted, and their lives are at least sometimes out of control around some substance such as alcohol or cocaine, or some process such as sex or gambling. Many Western cities appear, at least at times, overrun by the New Barbarians.

Second, these populations are increasingly similar to the populations that the movements of Patrick, Columba, and Aidan reached as the New Barbarians become increasingly postmodern. For more than two centuries, the ideology of the Enlightenment shaped the climate of modernity that profoundly shaped people's consciousness in the West. It scripted people to believe that they were essentially good and rational creatures; that they could build morality and society on reason alone; that science and education would deliver humanity from its problems; that progress was inevitable; and that the universe functions like a machine—a closed system leaving no need for the supernatural and little room for spirituality.[2]

As the Enlightenment has faded, postmodern people are increasingly suspicious of people and institutions that claim authority, and they are increasingly dubious of ultimate explanations. They are rediscovering their intuition, and they own and trust their feelings more. They take in the world through what they see, touch, and experience—not just through what they hear—and they explore spirituality and the supernatural.

The grounds of their identities are shifting. Prior to the Enlightenment, according to Martyn Atkins (now the secretary of British Methodism), people said, "I belong, therefore I am." Under the Enlightenment's influence, people said, "I think, therefore I am." Postmodern people now seem to be saying, "I feel, therefore I am," "I shop, therefore I am," "I look good, therefore I am," "I disobey, therefore I am," "I doubt, therefore I am," or "I am, so what?" We also observe the new tribalism of much of the West—as life in peer groups, subcultures, organizations, and ethnic groups produces an "I belong, therefore I am" source of identity once again.

Third, most churches assume, once again (though this is seldom verbalized), that the postmodern New Barbarians are unreachable because they are not cultured or civilized enough to become "real" Christians. Remarkably, most churches assume this in a time when the New Barbarians are often the most receptive people in our communities; many are searching for life, but "in all the wrong places."

So, at least 80 percent of our churches ignore two populations, year after year: the people who aren't "refined" enough to feel comfortable with us, and the people who are too "out of control" for us to feel comfortable with them! Several years ago, while consulting with a church, I did some laundry at the local Laundromat and visited with eight people. Seven were unchurched; six had never been involved in any church; five would be interested, however, if a church were interested in them. I took their names and addresses to the church leader group and heard this response: "The people who frequent that Laundromat aren't even nice."

So we can see enough parallels between the Celtic era and ours to understand the growing interest in Celtic Christianity. A renaissance in Celtic music, Celtic art, Celtic dance, Celtic love of nature, and Celtic spirituality is already under way. John Finney's *Recovering the Past* began the movement to help Western Christianity do evangelism and mission in more Celtic ways; the first edition of *The Celtic Way of Evangelism* contributed to that movement.

It is now possible to summarize some key strategic insights more cogently than before. In recent years, my field seminars have featured the top ten insights that can be introduced in a teaching session; one needs to "read the book" to nuance and fill out the ten points, and alas some other insights are gained only through reading and reflection. One day, I discovered that some alliteration helped seminar attendees and me to remember the points.

1. Credibility. The leaders of the ancient movement were perceived to live by, and even embody, the message they commended to the populations they reached.
2. Clearance. The movement's leaders knew to engage the local king and other opinion leaders to secure permission to camp next to the settlement.
3. Contact. As they camped next to the settlement, they befriended the people and spent the necessary time to understand the people and their beliefs, values, customs, issues, and struggles.

4. Community. Celtic Christianity was a communal version of the faith. Its leaders were formed in community, and they invited receptive people into the community—before they had yet experienced or believed much of anything.

5. Communication. The gospel is the message that makes faith possible; theology is (as Anselm taught us) "faith seeking understanding." Celtic Christianity demonstrated that it was possible to communicate the Christian treasure, to both pre-Christian and Christian people, with more imagination and in more ways than most churches have practiced.

6. Conversation. From the earliest biographies of Patrick, Aidan, and Cuthbert, we have learned that the ministry of conversation is the most important single way that the faith's meaning is communicated. Although the public presentation of Christianity is perennially necessary in the total communicative process, two-way conversation is more reproductive than one-way presentation.

7. Contextualization. The Celtic Christian movement did not impose one establishment-certified institutionalized expression of Christianity everywhere; they implemented the principle of "indigenous" Christianity before we knew what to call it, and the movement seems to have adapted to local cultures everywhere.

8. Continuity. In some contrast to the "slash and burn" approach of the earlier mission of Saint Martin of Tours, the Celtic movement built on whatever it could in the people's primal religion that preceded the introduction of Christianity.

9. Consistency. From all of the available data, Celtic Christianity spread in ways that are wholly consistent with the principles by which the Church grows in any time or context.

10. Conviction. Compared to more settled establishment Christianity, the Celtic movement was convinced that populations that were not like "good church people" could be reached if they approached them right and, in God's good time, would produce their fair share of apostles, prophets, saints, and martyrs.

Many Christian movements in the West, since the Celtic era, have based their strategic vision and approach on such themes. Whenever they are doing it, they are at least somewhat out of the mainline version of Christianity; they are an alternative expression of Christianity. Usually, though, it is difficult to tell whether the leaders discovered these as original ideas, whether they consciously plugged into Celtic Christian precedents, or whether they latched onto some of its themes (like imagination and hospitality) without regard to their probable Celtic source.[3] I usually guess the latter; these themes have resided somewhere in Western Christianity's ancestral memory ever since the tenth century and have resurfaced from time to time.

For example, eighteenth-century Methodism grew remarkably among England's "working poor" people who crowded into the cities during the Industrial Revolution. From the beginning of their time in the cities, they did not fit into the literate and refined culture of the Church of England, whose parish churches and cathedrals largely ignored their presence. John Wesley, however, went to great lengths, through observation, interviews, and correspondence, to understand England's unchurched populations. Methodism, like Celtic Christianity before it, took root and became contagious almost everywhere in the open air. Wesley's movement practiced the principles of hospitality and belonging-before-believing; the movement welcomed seekers into the fellowship of Methodist class meetings, and even into membership in Methodist societies, before they believed or had experienced anything.

Most of them "caught" the faith from the fellowship. Methodism was a lay movement that saw itself as an alternative community, that practiced the ministry of conversation, and that contextualized the message and addressed middle as well as ultimate issues. Methodist leaders were aware of the influence of ethos and pathos, and of the importance of identifying with the target population in communicating the message and in calling the people to a new identity.

Wesley traveled to communities with an apostolic band, which ministered as a team to a community, usually with the goal to plant a Methodist society or to start new classes within a society. Methodism formed its people in ways reminiscent of the Celtic approach. Methodism engaged people's imaginations through Charles Wesley's poetry and the folk arts of the people. Early Methodism employed an alternative architecture in which people felt comfortable, which was conducive to fellowship and to sensing the immanence of the triune God. Early Methodism adopted the people's kind of music, and many people sang their way into faith. Like the movement spawned by Patrick, Wesley's movement believed it had recovered the original apostolic mission to pre-Christian populations. Despite these (and other) similarities, and despite the fact that Wesley had read Bede's *Ecclesiastical History of the English People*, we cannot demonstrate that John Wesley was consciously appropriating themes from ancient Celtic Christianity. For the last thousand years, many Celtic ways have detached from their roots and freely circulated among the options that Christian leaders sometimes choose.

In the twentieth century, a number of academic fields validated what the Celtic Christian leaders knew intuitively or from experience. The Celtic understanding that you help people find faith and The Way by bringing them into Christian community, and into the ministry of conversation, has been strongly validated in the field of the sociology of knowledge. Peter Berger and Thomas Luck-mann's *The Social Construction of Reality*[4] features three major insights that especially validate the Celtic way: (1) a person's view of reality is largely shaped, and maintained, within the community into which one has been socialized; (2) in a pluralistic society, the possibility of conversion—that is, changing the way one perceives essential reality—is opened up through conversations with people who live with a contrasting view of reality; and (3) one adopts and internalizes the new worldview through resocialization into a community sharing that new worldview.

Once upon a time, only intuitive geniuses like Patrick and William Carey could make serious sense of other cultures, but the insights and categories of cultural anthropology have equipped almost anyone, with time and effort, to understand another culture. A culture is defined as the learned pattern of beliefs, attitudes, values, customs, and products shared by a people. A culture is sometimes explained, metaphorically, as "the software of the mind" that has been programmed into a given people's shared consciousness through their early socialization.

Culture exists at different levels. There are macro-cultures—like the Anglo, Arabic, Far Eastern, and sub-Saharan African macrocultures, with multiple cultures within each (such as English, Palestinian, Korean, and Masai cultures). Some cultural anthropologists estimate that there are fourteen macrocultures on earth, and about thirty thousand peoples—each with its own name, culture, and language or dialect. Furthermore, most people live within one or more specific subcultures—such as the Appalachian subculture, the baby boomer generational subculture, the horse-racing subculture, the fitness subculture, or the subculture of addiction—which extend across cultures and even across macrocultures.

People with addictions are among the most obvious, and least understood, New Barbarians in the West today.

Secular society glibly labels such people as "drunks," "pot-heads," or "losers," and it is oblivious to the fact that no one chooses to become addicted. It is ignorant of the physical origins of addiction and the psychological, spiritual, and cultural forces behind addiction. Often, church people glibly explain addiction as sin; then, as they (strangely) assume that the power of sin is greater than "the One who is in us" (see 1 John 4:4), they shun, withdraw from, or even excommunicate people hijacked by addiction. Meanwhile, the academic study of addiction, in fields like genetics, psychology, and cultural anthropology, has experienced enormous progress in understanding addiction.

Scholars now tell us, "An addiction is any substance or process that has taken over our lives and over which we are powerless."[5] One may become addicted to a "substance"— such as alcohol, drugs, nicotine, or even food. One may become addicted to a "process"—such as gambling, sex, relationships, or even a "religious high." Whatever the specific addiction, the addictive personalities become more self-centered; they lose touch with their feelings; and they experience ethical deterioration and, in time, spiritual bankruptcy. The addiction takes over their lives incrementally, from use to misuse to abuse to addiction.[6] Geneticists tell us that some people, perhaps one in eight, are born with a genetic predisposition toward addiction.

We have advanced in our understanding of the psychology of addiction. We know that denial is the fundamental defense mechanism of addiction; addicts typically deny what is obvious to everyone else in their lives. When confronted, addictive personalities deny, minimize, or rationalize their problem, or they live with the illusion that they are in control. They become liars in their relations with others, and with themselves; their memories become distorted; and like a tornado in the living room, they trigger chaos in the lives of the people who love them.

William L. White's *Pathways from the Culture of Addiction to the Culture of Recovery*[7] has demonstrated the astonishing complexity of addiction by showing that the addictive personality is sucked into a "tribe" or a "social world" that values, introduces, reinforces, and celebrates drug abuse and even shapes people over time into a different identity. For instance, the addiction tribe's new members acquire a new language and conversation themes while losing the capacity to talk about their feelings. They enter a new world of symbols—paraphernalia, logos, specific clothing or jewelry, and "articles associated with hustling behavior such as beepers."[8] Addicts become involved with institutions, places associated with abuse (like the saloons in towns of the old West), and with daily rituals that trigger abuse—such as using after meals or between activities, or more elaborate rituals like a needle-sharing ritual. The culture of addiction develops or uses music, like the rap music that legitimizes rage and glorifies cocaine use, that reaches repetitively into the addict's right brain to confirm the culture's beliefs and values, to make the drug lifestyle seem normal, and to trigger craving. The new recruit is gradually introduced to a local tribal history, which is

> passed on through stories and folktales. Most of these stories, which serve as a primary vehicle to transmit values, revolve around significant tribal events and personalities. "Hustling tales" become a way of transmitting knowledge and techniques to neophytes about various cons. Descriptions of heroes depicted in these tales become a way of shaping desired personality attributes of cultural members. "Copping tales" are used to teach neophytes the skills and dangers involved in procuring drugs. "Getting-off tales" convey a whole body of folklore and folk medicine on how to use and reduce risks associated with use. "Enemy tales" reinforce cultural paranoia and teach neophytes how to cope with cultural enemies, e.g., undercover agents, snitches, nonsmokers, supervisors, dealers who peddle "garbage," "shrinks," and "crazies."[9]

White describes some twenty different roles that the tribal members enact to support and expand the culture of addiction. For example, the "dealer" provides drugs of choice for the members. The "high priest" champions the culture's values and drug use and targets possible new converts. The "storyteller" is the culture's oral historian. The "medicine man" has folk remedies for hangovers, overdoses, and infections. The "jailhouse lawyer" helps members cope with law enforcement agencies and treatment professionals. The other roles, like the "hustler," the "ambassador," the "celebrity addict," the "crazies," and the "profiteers," reveal the remarkably sophisticated culture that undergirds the addictive lifestyle.

White reports that, in time, involvement with the drug and with the drug culture changes a person's identity and religious orientation. Whereas before drug use some persons were religious, some ignored religion, and some were emotionally rejecting their religious roots, such differences disappear as addiction takes over. Addiction does not make atheists or agnostics:

> Addiction, until the latest stages, renders questions of God and religion insignificant. . . . Addiction is so consuming there simply is no energy available to raise religious questions, let alone ponder answers. Addiction becomes one's religion, drugs become one's God, and rituals of use become rites of worship.[10]

Because "the total drug experience" is so social, consuming, and transformative, it is often more difficult to liberate a person from the addictive culture than from the drug. Indeed, membership and involvement in an alternative "culture of recovery" are usually necessary for a person's freedom from the twin powers of the drug and the drug culture.

Some of the same categories that describe the culture of addiction describe the culture of recovery. Bill White contends that changing one's language profoundly aids recovery.[11] Recovery involves shedding the conversation themes, jargon, profanity, hustling tales, and other features of "addictspeak," and acquiring conversation themes, language, and perspectives that help one make sense of one's experience and move into recovery and a renewed identity. Often, for example, the recovering addict will drop the nickname or alias of his or her drug culture experience and select another name. Likewise, people in recovery need to shed the symbols, daily rituals, music, and role models that fuel the addictive lifestyle (like converts from primal religions who burn their fetishes when converting to Christianity) and replace them with symbols, daily rituals, music, and role models that focus and empower recovery. One needs to say good-bye to the old institutions—that is, the "slippery places"—and hang out at healthy, drug-free havens. Recovery involves acquiring a new oral history and a larger story within which to understand one's life, and a new wisdom to guide one's life.

The culture of recovery exists and extends through people who play some twenty-one different roles. For example, the "high priest" is a person in recovery who skillfully and passionately articulates recovery principles to new members and to the outside world. The "elders" serve as role models for the life of sobriety and serenity. The "storyteller" is the culture's oral historian who teaches recovery values and wisdom through narrative; the "comedian" teaches and heals through humor. The "medicine man" is a folk healer. The "mentor" supports and guides people early in recovery.[12]

For most people, White says, recovery involves religious experience. Addictive people need to reconnect with their spirituality and with God and experience "rebirth"— defined (in part) as breakthrough in self-perception, decision to change, empowerment for new life, and the reconstruction of personal values.[13] For most people, all of this takes place within a recovery community.

A generation of addiction research has strongly validated the Celtic Christian awareness that we need to understand a "barbarian" population to reach and serve them, and also the Celtic confidence that we can understand them and reach them. Bill White's "culture of recovery" also validates the Celtic Christian emphasis on the role of community experience in people finding truth, life, and a new identity, and the role of daily rituals in reinforcing that identity. Increasing numbers of churches are liberating people from the culture of addiction by bringing them into an intentional Christian recovery community. Indeed, the 12-step movement is this generation's underground awakening.

The power of Christian recovery communities is best observed in people. I have interviewed many people who found deliverance from addiction's mysterious power through community involvement and religious experience. For instance, a great athlete in Southern California, in the 1970s, was featured in several movies until Hollywood passed him by. He fell into depression, and he self-medicated with booze, which led to alcoholism and a bed in an intensive care unit. The Holy Spirit visited him in the hospital and gave him the power to walk out of the hospital and away from alcohol. Since I knew that a single religious experience, by itself, might not liberate someone for life, I inquired, "What recovery community helps you stay in recovery?" He replied, "My church is my recovery community!" His story is exceptional only in the sequence of events. Most people get into the recovery community first and then experience the Higher Power.

Increasing numbers of churches are starting an alternative recovery congregation within the church. Some churches now begin as churches for the recovery population in the community. Other churches are transitioning into recovery churches.

Meredith Whitaker was (and still is) the leader of Cookson Hills Center, a United Methodist mission among Native American Indians in eastern Oklahoma, when, in 1990, she was asked to lead services each Sunday for the struggling Canterbury Chapel United Methodist Church in Vian, Oklahoma. For eighteen months, Meri Whitaker preached to two people (who ran off the occasional visitors!). Whitaker observed that many people in the community who were being helped in Alcoholics Anonymous groups needed to know more about God than the "Serenity Prayer," and they had nowhere to go to church.

Whitaker persuaded one of the two regular members to turn Canterbury Chapel into a recovery congregation; the other member left! While this decision cost Whitaker half of her entire congregation (!), they got the word out to the AA community, and twenty-seven people came on the first Sunday of Canterbury Chapel's new history.

Meri Whitaker indigenized the service to fit the Alcoholics Anonymous culture and experience. The service begins with Reinhold Neibuhr's famous "Serenity Prayer": "God, grant me the serenity to accept the things I cannot change, the courage to change the things I can, and the wisdom to know the difference." Whitaker often engages recovery issues in her sermons, and she features what the people need to know about God beyond the "Serenity Prayer." The service closes as the people join hands and pray together the Lord's Prayer. The church has a norm against coming to church dressed up; casual attire is expected, and Whitaker usually models the "casualization of Christianity" by leading the service wearing jeans.

In nineteen years, Canterbury Chapel has received almost two hundred new members; most were in recovery, and most had never gone to church before. Whitaker admits that, in ministry with a recovery population, you lose some people. Some people relapse; others move on. Nevertheless, the church thrives. Meanwhile, the contribution of Cookson Hills Center has expanded. When Meri Whitaker came as the mission's executive, the center had three buildings and a staff of one and a half; today, twenty staff members lead ministries in, and from, twenty buildings. She features the ministries and people of the church and the center in her book *My Sister, the Father*.

Meri Whitaker observes that most church people are like Jonah, who famously resisted his mission assignment to prophesy to the Ninevites; most church people actually assume that the "Ninevites" do not deserve God's love. Canterbury Chapel, however, wants the people who would not "fit" in most churches, and Meri reports that if someone cusses in church, "nobody gets bent out of shape!"

As Whitaker interprets the Canterbury Chapel's mission to other churches, she recalls the Sunday that a motorcycle gang of eight first visited the church. Before the benediction, one biker asked to say something: "I've been in prison for fifteen years. Damn, I didn't think I'd ever go to church, and I sure as hell didn't think I'd ever find a church that would have me. But I really need this." As she reports this incident to church leaders, Whitaker pauses to let the biker's words sink in and then says: "For those of you who are more concerned that I cussed in your church today than you are that there are people out there who think the church won't have them, I'm here to tell you—your priorities are all messed up."

The Canterbury Chapel story illustrates the first of two types of opportunities that many churches face. Some churches serve communities where many people are already in 12-step recovery groups but need a church. In most communities, however, there are far more people needing recovery than there are recovery groups with leaders-in-recovery to serve them; in these cases, churches are starting, and multiplying, recovery groups and congregations as explicit ministries of the church.

Indeed, some Christian movements are pioneering very intensive recovery communities. For instance, New Horizons Ministries organizes recovery communities in Marion, Indiana, as well as in Ontario, Canada, and the Dominican Republic. New Horizons specializes in ministry to "out of control" teenagers with attention deficit disorder (ADD), attention deficit/ hyperactivity disorder (ADHD), oppositional defiant disorder, addictive traits, or a pattern of self-destructive behaviors, whom parents and schools can no longer manage. New Horizons' community experiences involve structure, discipline, worship, Scripture study, prayer, group experiences, journaling, counseling, labor projects, and physical activities in a natural wilderness setting. Tim Blossom, New Horizons' director, reports that students especially grow from the camaraderie they experience from helping one another, and from their service with poor people or with self-destructive children. The process takes months, but many teens find a new identity and a new life through such community experience. Tim Blossom reports that New Horizons, which began in 1971, was the pioneer in such ministry; today there are more than five hundred such ministries in the United States.

The second half of the twentieth century experienced a widespread renewal of many other features of Celtic Christianity. Ian Bradley observes that some of the most influential Christian writers of the twentieth century, like John Baillie, Pierre Teilhard de Chardin, and Thomas Merton, were drawing from a distinctively Celtic theological vision.[14] Vincent Donovan's reflection in *Christianity Rediscovered* views his years as "the Apostle to the Masai" through profoundly perceptive Celtic lenses. Celtic spirituality now has many public leaders. I am told that Trinity College in Dublin, Cliff College, and the universities of Wales, Aberdeen, St. Andrews, Glasgow, Edinburgh, Durham, and Cambridge offer one or more degree programs in Celtic studies, though not exclusively in Christian

Celtic studies. I am told that the new monasticism, the Taizé community in France, and many of the emerging churches, missional churches, and apostolic experiments in the West have conscious Celtic roots.

In 1938, George MacLeod rediscovered several Celtic Christian themes. He led the movement that restored the medieval abbey at Iona, Columba's ancient headquarters, and he launched the Iona Community as a force for church renewal and justice, prayer and healing, and mission and evangelization.[15] Following MacLeod's death, the Iona Community dropped his interest in evangelization and redefined mission around causes like peace, justice, ecology, urban ministry, gay and lesbian causes, and interfaith dialogue—though I could find no records of the Iona Community actually participating in interfaith dialogues. Iona is an inspiring place to visit, and it has a useful library, but I met no one on the staff who knew much about Celtic Christianity or who sympathized with Celtic evangelical mission.

The Holy Island of Lindisfarne is moving in the opposite direction. David Adam, the rector of Holy Island, is the most prolific writer of devotional literature in the Celtic tradition. Ray Simpson now leads the Retreat Center at Lindisfarne and heads the Society of Aidan and Hilda—with a growing membership in Britain and beyond. Kate Tristram retired early as a professor of church history at the University of Durham to head Marygate House at Lindisfarne, where she built a significant Celtic library. She may be the most articulate interpreter of Celtic Christian history.

Many churches today, such as Revelation Church in Chichester, England, are consciously informed by a Celtic Christian vision. Revelation's leaders know that most postmodern people experience "belonging before believing," so they welcome the full involvement of seekers. Their goal is to plant churches so indigenous to each people group "that its expression will emerge from within their culture, in their language, styles and flavours, yet still embodying the counter-cultural values of the gospel."[16] Revelation Church involves its people in soul friendships, small groups, lay ministries, the ministry of witness, and cross-cultural mission. It features ministries for people who are deaf, addicted, or disabled. Revelation Church has planted churches in Portsmouth and Bognor Regis; it supports missionaries in Tanzania, Zambia, and Mongolia, and projects in several other countries. Most of Revelation Church's ministries are lay-led, and three of the seven people on the leadership team are women. Revelation Church is discovering ways to communicate through visual symbols and the creative arts. The movement's leaders report:

> At times, within the context of our worship meetings, we have encouraged artists to come and draw what they feel is happening as the church worships together. We have also had sculptors and even potters working to one side of the meeting. Sometimes, in the process of the worship the artists are encouraged to interpret what it is they are portraying. At other times the work is left to stand in its own right and people are invited to go and view it at the end and ask the Holy Spirit to speak to them.[17]

The Jesus Movement in Australia is also consciously Celtic in its roots and vision. The movement began around 1970, under the leadership of John Smith, as an outbreak of indigenous evangelistic and prophetic activity in Irish pubs, coffee shops, arts communities, folk music communities, and hippie communities, and in debates on race and justice on university campuses. The movement evolved into an apostolic order in cooperation with several Australian denominations. The Australian Jesus Movement targeted people in (and beyond) the fringes of establishment society, such as bikers, hippies, naturalists, addictive people, alienated young people, apocalyptic people expecting the end of the world, and the wandering seekers who were experimenting with Eastern religions like Zen. Smith reports that the movement wanted "anyone who felt marginalized and alienated from the established culture." Occasionally, whole communities—such as the Garden Island Creek settlement in Tasmania—turned to Christian faith.

Smith would organize an apostolic team of a dozen to thirty or more people to engage a community for some days. Team members let their hair grow, traveled on motorcycles, and, when appropriate, wore hippie shirts or leather jackets. Many team members were etched with Celtic Christian tattoos, which, Smith recalls, "stimulated questions everywhere!" After evening services, groups infiltrated bars and taverns to befriend, converse with, and invite people. If a team was reaching out in its own city, as many as one hundred people would fan out and engage pubs, art centers, and other locations where people converse. When on the road, they usually ministered with, and at the invitation of, the churches already in the community, with the goal of starting new groups and ministries for, say, men, youth, or people with addictions. Where it was impossible to assimilate converts and active seekers into existing churches, the movement would start a new Saint Martin's Community Church.

Saint Martin's Community Churches are experiments in indigenous Australian Christianity, especially for Irish immigrant populations in Australia, and are based on a perceptive analysis of the Irish cultural personality. John Smith observes, "The Irish know how to celebrate—with minimum resources and with minimum reasons (in the world's terms) to celebrate." One might almost guess, Smith muses, that the Irish are genetically encoded to be celebratory personalities. Furthermore, the Irish celebrate more or less the same, "whether in the pub, or the church, or the wake! They enjoy a joke on the deceased! And they enjoy a joke in church." Irish Christians, Smith says, see the kingdom of God in part "as a party—where the doors are thrown open like an Irish pub to anyone who would come in." So Smith believes that church should feel something like an Irish pub—festive, lyrical, participatory—with everyone welcome. "No one is going to check your credentials. Leave your attitude at the door, come in, find your place, and feel free to express your gift."

Though each Saint Martin's church is somewhat different from the others, the first one, in Melbourne, is illustrative. The walls are of mud brick—in the Aussie outback bush tradition. Thick planks, hewn from Australian gum trees, provide the vertical support. The sanctuary features two open fireplaces to suggest the church is a "house" of God. Soup is cooking in the large pot behind the podium, which will provide the communal meal that concludes the service. There is no baptistery; the movement baptizes converts in the nearby river—as a public event and an opportunity to publicly declare and dramatize the gospel. Volunteers largely built the church; a team of women made all the mud bricks. Some volunteers were seekers. The man who cut the gum tree planks was a seeker, and Smith recalls, "We saw him growing like a plant in the sun."

Saint Martin's worship is, most of all, unrestrained, uninhibited celebration, more or less "in the tradition of an Irish pub," Smith says. The services are long, by usual standards, and many of their people have short attention spans; six or eight people with schizophrenia may attend a service. Consequently, people are often entering and exiting the service or getting up and walking over for coffee. The spirit of unpredictability hangs in the air!

Services feature clear and relevant biblical preaching, which faces both the ultimate issues and the daily middle issues. Services encourage emotional self-expression and "the full expression of one's soul." Services feature storytelling because Smith believes that "story engages deeply the Irish spirit—and all human spirits." The church's staple music is reminiscent of the Irish ballad, though they also include ancient Christian music, ancient and contemporary Celtic music, and music from other Christian traditions and cultures.

Saint Martin's church encourages the full expression of the Christian imagination and often features indigenous art, much of it postmodern (sometimes extreme), serving Christian themes. Wall hangings are often featured around the sanctuary, with perhaps a cross surrounded with barbed wire at the front. Once the leaders invited, and displayed, a hundred art pieces on the Crucifixion. One featured a slaughtered lamb; another showed the dying man's genitalia—which, of course, reflected what crucifixion actually looked like; full exposure was one source of the public shame of crucifixion.

Some liturgies, especially during Advent and Lent, are rooted in very ancient traditions, but Saint Martin's worship is more noteworthy for its spontaneity, openness, and inclusiveness. For example, pedophiles are welcomed in the church; they are "accompanied" when they visit a restroom or a children's area. Each service is planned, but Smith recalls, "We will put the plan aside if it's necessary, for a redemptive moment." Once a man walked into a service while holding a can of beer and cursing. The service changed pace, welcomed him, and drew him in, and today he is a "regular."

John Smith, like the ancient Celtic apostles, believes that affirmation and paradox, understanding and mystery, are all important in theology. He believes that some truth is expressed better through metaphor and artistry than through theological propositions. He believes that we should "do church" in ways that are "ancient and liturgical, and also postmodern, spontaneous, and a bit profane." He believes that "sensuality and spirituality should be friends." In outreach, Smith reflects on the movement's adoption of hippie shirts, tattoos, and so on, but warns that "you can't ape it or go native. Your heart has to be in it and really identifying with the people so much that you have common cause with the indigenous people," as in their love for nature or their quest for justice. Smith remembers, "They became our people. We joined in common cause with them." He especially believes in involving seekers in the community's fellowship and celebration. "Often," he reports, "we didn't know when evangelism ended and mutual celebration began."

Some Christian movements, such as the Alpha course from Holy Trinity Church in the Brompton section of London, are more or less unconsciously informed by a Celtic Christian vision. The Alpha course served, for more than a decade, as Holy Trinity's introduction to Christianity for seekers who want to "sniff around," "kick the tires," check out Christianity, and try it on for size. In the early 1990s, the church's leaders introduced other church leaders to the course, and its growth has been remarkable—from 5 registered courses in 1992, to 10,500 in 72 countries in 1998, to 33,500 courses in 163 countries in 2008. Churches in all major theological traditions, from Methodist, Baptist, Lutheran, and Presbyterian to Anglican, Orthodox, and Roman Catholic, now employ Alpha courses to engage pre-Christian people.

A seeker attends an Alpha course for most of a season— one session a week for ten weeks, climaxed by a weekend retreat covering the last four sessions. The seeker discovers that she or he is an honored "guest" of a church that practices the ministry of hospitality. The seeker's experience, each session, begins with fellowship around a meal, followed by a welcome, a time of celebrative worship, a talk,[18] refreshments, and then a conversation time in a small group of eight to twelve people.

Alpha's leaders observe that through the Alpha experience seekers are partly socialized into Christian belief, and the small-group experience is indispensable in this socialization process. A group's leader functions essentially as a host and conversation facilitator rather than a teacher, and the seekers are treated like guests rather than auditors or pupils. Within several weeks, the group leader has developed a pastoral care relationship with group members—encouraging people, praying for people, praying with people, and inviting (without pressure) response to the Holy Spirit. Each week, group members ask their questions, express their ideas and feelings, and discuss Christianity's possibilities for their lives. Frequently the group bonds and continues meeting as a group long after the Alpha course is completed. Most of Holy Trinity Church's new groups emerge from the Alpha courses, and most of the church's new leaders experience their initial development as group leaders; indeed, new converts often lead a group in the very next Alpha course.

The curriculum's theology is patently trinitarian; the presentations are filled with humor, analogies, and other expressions from imagination to imagination and from heart to heart. People experience the last four sessions, on the Holy Spirit, in a weekend retreat in a natural setting—because people are more likely to experience the Holy Spirit in nature.

The Alpha movement has raised up staff and laity to reach many New Barbarians for Alpha experiences. For instance, Bob Byrne lived a life of addiction, crime, and violence before a Christian woman explained the fish symbol on her lapel. She invited him to follow Christ and to learn how through an Alpha course. Today, he is a theology graduate, an Anglican priest, and he leads Alpha courses for people who "society says are no good." He says,

I see people from all walks of life who don't know God and I know that is the most precious thing that they could possibly find.

I like working with people nobody else wants to work with—people with drug problems, people who society says are no good. I do a lot of work in schools.

My favorite kids are always the worst kids, because everyone else says they can't do anything with them. They are right: they can't, but God can.

That's why I love Alpha so much. The beautiful thing about Alpha is that it digs and builds a foundation.[19]

An issue of *Alpha News* reported Alpha courses in more than a hundred prisons across the United Kingdom and announced courses to be offered in all prisons in Texas. One story features a former male model in the fashion industry who experienced God's grace, made sense of the experience from an Alpha course at Holy Trinity Church, and is now involved in volunteer ministry with the families of AIDS victims. Another story features a young man set free from drugs and the drug culture through his Alpha community experience. Still another story features a middle-aged man who experienced recovery from alcohol addiction in a 12-step program a decade ago but still experienced "a great big hole inside of me." The Holy Spirit filled that hole during the final weekend retreat of an Alpha course.

Although there are numerous parallels between ancient Celtic Christianity and the contemporary Alpha course, in interviews with the pastors responsible for the course—Sandy Millar and Nicky Gumbel—they reported no conscious appropriation of any models or insights from Celtic Christianity. It is possible that the original developer of the Alpha course, no longer on Holy Trinity's staff, was drawing on the Celtic Christian tradition. It is also possible that Holy Trinity, like increasing numbers of churches, has picked up some pieces of the Celtic way of doing church without conscious regard to their historic source.

Some of the Celtic Christian movement's achievements

might not seem very achievable today, such as the way that their monastic communities created a center for community in the midst of rural sprawl. We find today, however, many cases of urban sprawl, and one of the secrets of the American megachurch has been its capacity to create a center for community in the midst of urban sprawl. If you flew over our section of metropolitan Lexington, Kentucky, for instance, you would detect no obvious pattern, plan, or center for community in this metropolitan region; you would see only a random patchwork of housing estates, subdivisions, horse farms, shops, and so on.

Southland Christian Church, in our region, has become a megachurch averaging more than seven thousand in attendance that provides a place for community in the midst of urban sprawl. In this region of the city, if you attend a concert or a play; if your teenager attends a private high school or is in a youth group; if you give blood or vote for a jailer or a president; if you play softball or your child is a Boy Scout or Girl Scout or plays soccer; if you do aerobics or attend a support group or study conversational Spanish; if you need an appliance or a piece of furniture or some vegetables—you probably come to Southland Christian Church.

The two most prominent Celtic approaches to evangelization—a monastic community welcoming seekers as guests, and teams from the monastic community visiting settlements for weeks or months—might, at first blush, seem unavailable to churches today. None of us live in Celtic monastic communities, and it is not vocationally possible for most of us to relocate in teams for blocks of time. This is a case in which the specific models cannot be replicated, but the principles can be applied in new, relevant ways. The members of a number of intentional Christian communities, such as Dieter Zander's Re-Imagine Community in San Francisco, have "adopted" a neighborhood or region of the city and have moved in to live among the people.

Actually, most local churches are called to create more intentional ministries of hospitality than they have yet considered. My colleague at Asbury, Dr. Christine Pohl, wrote her dissertation in Christian ethics on the history of hospitality in the Christian tradition, and she has followed it with contemporary studies. She reports that her list of local churches who take hospitality seriously, and exercise it effectively, is short but growing. Some parachurch Christian communities, like the L'Abri fellowships, have given it serious attention, but most local churches have not. The typical hospitality ritual in a church goes no deeper than inviting guest worshipers to sign the registration pad so someone from the church can visit them later and maybe put a ribbon or a "guest" badge on their lapel in case someone wants to greet them.

I have learned, through interview research, that most pre-Christian visitors to a church feel anxious and vulnerable as they visit foreign turf, but often something is going on in their lives that they think a church might help with. Most church leaders, however, have never taken seriously the nonverbal communication that a visiting seeker is sending out. The seeker's visit is the most misperceived (or ignored) signal in local churches today, and the church's most neglected opportunity to reach receptive people. Often, following their visit, visitors feel ignored, judged, misunderstood, or unwanted, and they may conclude that God doesn't understand or want them either.

One type of church, the Cell-Driven Church (or the Church of Small Groups),[20] appears to have effective ways to help seekers experience hospitality. For instance, in the years of Dale Galloway's leadership at New Hope Community Church in Portland, Oregon, more than five hundred lay-led small groups met each week. Each small group had a symbolic empty chair to fill every six months, so members regularly invited people to visit their group, and these groups were primed and skilled to include new people.

Some churches, like the Brooklyn Tabernacle, may schedule a five- to ten-minute period in the worship service when people spontaneously gather into groups of four or five, exchange names, share something that is going on in their lives, and pray for one another. Somewhat like the Celtic Christians of old, some churches deploy teams in ministry and witness to identifiable communities. New York City has thousands of communities of people who are found, more or less, in some specific location. The Brooklyn Tabernacle especially targets some of the New Barbarian populations who live or congregate in specific known places—homeless people, street people, addicted people, drug pushers, exotic dancers, female prostitutes, male prostitutes, and so on. In any season, the Brooklyn Tabernacle sends out several teams of people to several targeted locations—a homeless shelter or a school bus parking area where male prostitutes sleep in the summer. The teams visit at the same time each week for a season or two. They engage in appropriate ministry, conversation, and prayer, and they invite people to a Brooklyn Tabernacle worship service.

Some churches and denominations use teams of people for church planting once again. Indeed, C. Peter Wagner reports that "hiving off" is "the most common way of planting a daughter church."[21] In this model, an "apostolic team" of people from one church will join a church planter to reach a target community, in the same city or area, to plant a new church.

"Colonization" is a more radical expression of the same principle. This model requires that the people pull up roots and find new jobs, homes, and schools in the target community.[22] My colleague at Asbury, Dr. Ron Crandall, tells me that some traditions—from Mennonites to Moravians—typically plant churches using a colonizing team. Dr. Charles Chaney reports that a Southern Baptist team of eleven laity from Amarillo, Texas, moved with Pastor

Frank Radcliff to the Chicago area and started a church in Oak Park. Then they targeted the suburb of Woodridge, and ten more people moved from Amarillo to join them; within three years the Woodridge Church averaged more than one thousand in attendance. In the following years, they planted additional churches for African Americans, Hispanics, and Filipinos.[23]

Some features of the ancient Celtic Christian movement are as relevant today as ever but, to my knowledge, are not currently implemented. For instance, the Celtic bishops were primarily evangelists rather than administrators; I know of no denomination with a missional job description for its bishops.

Some relevant Celtic Christian features are only occasionally expressed. For instance, I have interviewed people who have a soul friend without knowing what to call him or her. We occasionally observe a recovery of the Celtic love for nature in Christian communities, but (tragically, for our witness with "tree huggers") more often outside Christian communities. The proposal that we can reach people through their imaginations has been advanced in good books by Fred Craddock, Ralph Lewis, and Joe Harding, but not many Protestant churches have discovered the communicative power of poetry, story, or the visual arts. (Indeed, a majority of churches have not yet discovered that it is OK to make church interesting!)

Perhaps 10 to 20 percent of America's churches are trying culturally relevant "contemporary" worship, with some adaptation to the pre-Christian population's style, language, aesthetics, and music; more churches feature "blended" worship, which increases the number of people who find something they cannot relate to! Few churches, however, are even considering the kind of identification with people practiced by the Celtic Christian movement and reflected in this ancient Chinese poem:

Go to the people.
Live among them.
Learn from them.
Love them.
Start with what they know.
Build on what they have.[24]

Few churches have yet discovered what Celtic Christian leaders knew about Paul Hiebert's "excluded middle." Richard Mouw, president of Fuller Theological Seminary, contends that Western churches are called to help people understand

> God's day-to-day dealings with us in the midst of our practical uncertainties about, for example, our health, our financial resources, and our intimate relationships. When we fail to provide such an account, people—ordinary Christians— will turn to those elements of folk religion, such as new age.[25]

Mouw also contends that one reason for the success of some televangelists and megachurch pastors is their sensitivity to "excluded middle" questions and concerns.[26]

Most churches still attempt to do evangelism (if they attempt it at all) by bringing in a professional or by reaching out as individuals; the Celtic way of team ministry and outreach is seldom tried but is much more reproductive. Most attempts at evangelism today still emphasize a one-way presentation rather than the ministry of (two-way) conversation. Ray Simpson and Kate Tristram have adapted Saint Aidan's conversational approach to people to make it useful to any Christian reaching out. You engage people with a question like: "Are you a Christian?" or "Where do you stand with regard to the Christian faith?" If they say they are Christians, you ask, "How could you be a better one?" If they say they are not, you ask, "May I tell you something about it?"[27] and that begins a conversation.

The Celtic strategy of sending teams into "enemy territory" is almost never done today, but it is the greatest apostolic adventure available to most Christians. Indeed, in the great "silent retrenchment" of the last third of the twentieth century, most churches ceased doing much proactive outreach at all. In most cities, most of the growing churches are only responding to people who take the initiative to visit the church.

Finally, not many churches are yet following Christ to reach the receptive New Barbarians who are all around us. That is tragic because, deep down, most of these people want to experience God's forgiveness and acceptance; they would like a second chance and a new life. The Church has what most people are looking for, but the Church is not offering it to them! Nevertheless, the Celtic Christian movement that won the West for a second time has shown us many ways for reaching the West for a third time—if we have the eyes to see, and if we can rediscover that lost people matter to God.

The supreme key to reaching the West again is the key that Patrick discovered—involuntarily but providentially. The gulf between church people and unchurched people is vast, but if we pay the price to understand the unchurched, we will usually know what to say and what to do. If they know and feel we understand them, by the tens of millions they will risk opening their hearts to the God who understands them.

Notes

1. The Gospel to the Irish

1. John T. McNeill, *The Celtic Churches: A History* A.D. *200 to 1200* (Chicago and London: University of Chicago Press, 1974), p. 57.

2. From Liam de Paor's translation of "St. Patrick's Declaration," in Liam de Paor, *Saint Patrick's World: The Christian Culture of Ireland's Apostolic Age* (Notre Dame, Ind.: University of Notre Dame Press, 1993), p. 99.

3. Ibid., p. 100.

4. Virtually no two scholars are able to agree on Saint Patrick's key dates! R. P. C. Hanson presents the most comprehensive and judicious discussion that I have found. Essentially, Hanson calculates probable dates upon external evidence. For instance, Patrick's career presumably took place after the translation and dissemination of the version of the Bible that he uses and before the conversion of the Franks, whom Patrick refers to as pagans in his "Letter against the Soldiers of Coroticus." By such reasoning, Hanson pegs Patrick's birth around 390, his kidnapping in 406, his escape in 412, and his death around 460. Hanson estimates that Patrick went to Ireland as an apostolic bishop sometime between 425 and 435. (So, the traditional date for Patrick's entry into Ireland, 432, is as good as any other for the purposes of this study.) See R. P. C. Hanson, *Saint Patrick: His Origins and Career* (New York and Oxford: Oxford University Press, 1968), pp. 171–88.

5. R. Pierce Beaver, "The History of Mission Strategy," in Ralph D. Winter and Steven C. Hawthorne, eds., *Perspectives on the World Christian Movement*, rev. ed. (Pasadena, Calif.: William Carey Library, 1992), p. B–66.

6. Ibid., p. B–59.

7. Quoted in Beaver, "The History of Mission Strategy," p. B–62.

8. Ibid., p. B–65.

9. William Barclay, *The Master's Men* (Nashville: Abingdon Press, 1959). See also George G. Hunter III, *How to Reach Secular People* (Nashville: Abingdon Press, 1992), pp. 108–9.

10. Ralph Winter shows that, repeatedly, when the Roman Church refused to reach the "barbarians," the "barbarians" assaulted Rome. So, when the Church neglected outreach to the Goths, the Goths proceeded to overwhelm the Church and the "Christian" lands. Later, the neglected Vikings overwhelmed the churched lands. Still later, the invasions of Muslim armies wreaked havoc in Christian lands. See Ralph D. Winter, "The Kingdom Strikes Back: The Ten Epochs of Redemptive History," in Winter and Hawthorne, *Perspectives on the World Christian Movement*, pp. B–3 to B–21.

11. See Nigel Pennick, *The Sacred World of the Celts* (New York: Harper-Collins, 1997), p. 10.

12. Brendan Lehane, *The Quest of Three Abbots: The Golden Age of Celtic Christianity* (New York: Viking, 1968), p. 8.

13. Thomas Cahill, *How the Irish Saved Civilization: The Untold Story of Ireland's Heroic Role from the Fall of Rome to the Rise of Medieval Europe* (New York: Doubleday, 1995), p. 82. Nora Chadwick, *The Celts*, rev. ed. (New York: Penguin Books, 1997), p. 138. Cahill explains, "In warfare, as in so many other aspects of Celtic life, there appear to have been superficial overtones, as is suggested by the gaesatae who fought naked in obedience to an archaic ritual tradition which apparently taught that nudity afforded some supernatural protection." That deeper meaning behind a nude army's appearance would not have been apparent to opposing armies!

14. See Nora Chadwick, *The Celts*, pp. 53, 139.

15. Ibid., pp. 154–55.

16. Patrick, in the years of his enslavement, would have discovered that the Celts had a far more sophisticated and even civilized culture than their public image suggested. He became familiar with their art, music, poetry, and storytelling, and their laws, myths, and religion. Patrick knew that the Irish Celts were nonliterate by choice; they valued their strength as an oral and rather intellectual culture. Their lawyers and their bards (the storytellers who perpetuated their oral history) trained for twelve years; their Druids trained for twenty years.

17. Ian Bradley, *Columba: Pilgrim and Penitent* (Glasgow: Wild Goose Publications, 1996), p. 20.

18. De Paor, *Saint Patrick's World*, p. 23.

19. See Lehane, *The Quest of Three Abbots*, chap. 2.

20. Ibid., p. 42.

21. I found four ancient sources most useful—St. Patrick's "Declaration" and his "Letter against the Soldiers of Coroticus," Muirchu's "Life of St. Patrick," and Tirechan's seventh-century collection of local traditions about Patrick's mission. All of these sources, and others, are now

in excellent English translation and in one volume: de Paor's *Saint Patrick's World*.

22. This reflects the company of people who accompanied Patrick to Selc in Tirechan's collection of local traditions about Patrick's mission (see de Paor, *Saint Patrick's World*, p. 166). On another occasion, Patrick's entourage consisted of "a crowd of priests, deacons, exorcists, porters and lectors, as well as boys whom he ordained" (p. 155).

23. Louis Gougaud, who wrote a comprehensive pioneering text on Celtic Christianity in the 1930s, tells us that "we find Patrick everywhere setting himself first of all to convert the great." One reason, Gougaud says, for focusing on the king was that the king owned all the property, so the king had to give the land needed for a church. See Louis Gougaud, *Christianity in Celtic Lands: A History of the Churches of the Celts, Their Origin, Their Development, Influence, and Mutual Relations* (London: Sheed & Ward, 1932; repr., Dublin: Four Courts Press, 1992), pp. 38–39.

24. "Bishop Tirechan's Account of St. Patrick's Journey," in de Paor's *Saint Patrick's World*, pp. 163–65, seems to represent one such public conversation as typical of Patrick's approach.

25. We do not know if the Christian band would have offered the Eucharist to seekers, but I would not be astonished to learn that they did. Much later, John Wesley and eighteenth-century Methodism were to view the sacrament as a converting ordinance and welcome seekers to the Lord's Supper.

26. "Bishop Tirechan's Account of St. Patrick's Journey," in de Paor's *Saint Patrick's World*, p. 163.

27. James Bulloch, *The Life of the Celtic Church* (Edinburgh: Saint Andrew Press, 1963), p. 49.

28. We think that these provisional settlements seldom exceeded three hundred people. If tribes averaged three thousand people, then a tribe would be dispersed in, say, a dozen settlements in the same region.

29. In de Paor's *Saint Patrick's World*, p. 129.

30. Gougaud, *Christianity in Celtic Lands*, pp. 44–45. A few scholars are less impressed with Patrick and his alleged achievements. The most deconstructionist, and hostile, is E. A. Thompson, *Who Was Saint Patrick?* (Rochester, N.Y.: Boydell Press, 1985). Thompson criticizes what he views as Patrick's

> narrow conception of the aims of his mission. He aimed to convert the pagans, to bring them to the point of baptism, and, having baptized them, to move on to deal with persons who were still pagan. He might even leave new converts for his clergy to baptize and exhort, while he himself hurried on elsewhere. His aim, in fact, seems to have been to "convert" the maximum number of pagans. It almost amounts to a counting of heads.

Two or three times he tells us that the number of his converts amounted to "thousands." Sometimes it would seem that it was numbers alone which counted, not the results of conversion, not the effect on the lives of the converted. . . . Having converted one group (we might think), he rushes on to the next. (pp. 150–51)

Thompson believes that Patrick should have spent his priority time on worthier causes, like ransoming captives, rather than converting people from their religion to Christianity. Thompson paints Patrick as a modern "Lone Ranger" Elmer Gantry evangelist and seems oblivious to Patrick's team approach to settlements, the role of cross-cultural analysis and witness, the time they spent with a people, and a dozen other factors.

Thompson appears to have no firsthand experience with any Christian movement, with any other culture than his own, or with any other model of evangelization than some twentieth-century revival model that he dislikes. His trashing of Patrick is an inexpensive shot from an academic ivory tower. Thompson reveals his Enlightenment bias in one of his few "positive" comments about Patrick: "He never claims to have perpetrated a miracle" (p. 154).

Remarkably, Thompson also claims that Patrick "left no model to future generations. He had no successors in the sense that no one learned from him: no one launched missions similar to his outside other frontiers in imitation of him" (p. 157). This book's perspective contrasts with Thompson's by 180 degrees. There were hosts of successors who reached the rest of Ireland, Scotland, much of England, and much of Europe by doing more or less what he did.

31. Cahill, *How the Irish Saved Civilization*, p. 110.

32. From "St. Patrick's Declaration" in de Paor's *Saint Patrick's World*, pp. 103–4.

2. A New Kind of Community, a New Kind of Life

1. Gilbert Márkus, "Rooted in the Tradition," *Christian History* 60 (1998): 20.

2. Liam de Paor, *Saint Patrick's World: The Christian Culture of Ireland's Apostolic Age* (Notre Dame, Ind.: University of Notre Dame Press, 1993), p. 95.

3. James Bulloch, in *The Life of the Celtic Church* (Edinburgh: Saint Andrew Press, 1963), p. 49, believes Patrick began planting monastic communities very early in his Irish mission.

4. For such background insights, see de Paor's *Saint Patrick's World*, p. 23.

5. Philip Sheldrake, in *Living between Worlds: Place and Journey in Celtic Spirituality* (Boston: Cowley Publications, 1996), acknowledges the common assumption that Celtic monastic communities were usually located "in wild and isolated places" (p. 22), but he demonstrates that the location was usually selected for access, not for seclusion. Indeed, he contends, "Nearly all the major sites that grew into important monasteries are in fact on major travel routes or at least, in terms of ancient geography, in relatively accessible places" (p. 28).

6. Brigid in Ireland and Hilda in England were the two most notable abbesses of large monastic communities.

7. John Finney, *Recovering the Past: Celtic and Roman Mission* (London: Darton, Longman & Todd, 1996), p. 50.

8. In time, some of the great European universities emerged from these monastic communities.

9. *The Book of Kells* (on exhibit at Trinity College, Dublin) and *The Lindisfarne Gospels* are the most famous examples of this unique Celtic Christian art called "illumination." The Bible was the only book upon which a monastic community's artists practiced the art of illumination, which indicates their reverence for the Scriptures as God's unique revelation.

10. This picture of Celtic monastic communities is, necessarily, general. Brendan Lehane suggests, "Individual abbots made rules, which were sometimes adhered to and quite often not; some monasteries became lively centres of learning, some took on the duties of social service. There was no central authority, no unified aim, and the story of each community is different from that of others." *The Quest of Three Abbots: The Golden Age of Celtic Christianity* (New York: Viking, 1968), p. 17.

11. Sheldrake, *Living between Worlds*, pp. 38–39.

12. Ibid., p. 44.

13. Paul G. Hiebert, "The Flaw of the Excluded Middle," *Missiology: An International Review* 10, no. 1 (January 1982): 35–47. The article is reprinted more recently in Hiebert's book *Anthropological Reflections on Missiological Issues* (Grand Rapids: Baker Books, 1994), pp. 189–201.

14. Hiebert, "The Flaw of the Excluded Middle," p. 197.

15. Ibid.

16. I have oversimplified Hiebert's theory. He also shows that people tend to view each of the three levels from either a "mechanical" or an "organic" perspective. But that level of complexity is beyond what I need for this study.

17. Alexander Carmichael, *Carmina Gadelica: Hymns and Incantations* (Edinburgh: Floris Books, 1992). Used by permission of Floris Books.

18. Ray Simpson, "Contemplative Prayer," chap. 4 in *Exploring Celtic Spirituality: Historic Roots for Our Future* (London: Hodder & Stoughton, 1995), pp. 51–56.

19. Carmichael, *Carmina Gadelica*, p. 93.

20. Ibid., p. 35.

21. Ibid., p. 299.

22. Ibid., p. 217.

23. Ray Simpson, ed., *Celtic Blessings for Everyday Life: Prayers for Every Occasion* (London: Hodder & Stoughton, 1998).

24. Ibid., p. 5. Copyright © 1998 by Ray Simpson. Reproduced by permission of Hodder & Stoughton Limited.

25. Louis Gougaud, *Christianity in Celtic Lands: A History of the Churches of the Celts, Their Origin, Their Development, Influence, and Mutual Relations* (London: Sheed & Ward, 1932; repr., Dublin: Four Courts Press, 1992), p. 65.

3. To the Picts, the Anglo-Saxons, and Other "Barbarians"

1. The Irish Gaelic version of his name, which writers often use today, is Columcille.

2. Edward Sellner, *Wisdom of the Celtic Saints* (Notre Dame, Ind.: Ave Maria Press, 1993), p. 92.

3. Ian Bradley, *The Celtic Way* (London: Darton, Longman & Todd, 1993), p. 21.

4. See *The Coming of Christianity to Anglo-Saxon England* (London: B. T. Batsford, 1972), p. 26. See pp. 22–30 for Mayr-Harting's full discussion of Anglo-Saxon paganism.

5. John Finney, *Recovering the Past: Celtic and Roman Mission* (London: Darton, Longman & Todd, 1996), p. 65.

6. Ibid., p. 55.

7. See bk. 2 of Bede, *The Ecclesiastical History of the English Nation*, trans. by L. C. Jane (New York: E. P. Dutton, 1910) for Bede's account of the ministry of Paulinus. Bede reports on the later ministry of Aidan in bk. 3.

8. Mayr-Harting, *The Coming of Christianity to Anglo-Saxon England*, p. 29.

9. James Bulloch, in *The Life of the Celtic Church* (Edinburgh: Saint Andrew Press, 1963), p. 64, judges that "Augustine's success was practically confined to the southeast corner of England. Bishops were appointed to the sees of Canterbury, Rochester, and London, but even these dioceses had to struggle for existence." While some writers are most interested in the movement of Aidan in reaching Northumbria (the

largest of England's early medieval kingdoms), Bulloch estimates that "all England north of the Thames was indebted to the Celtic mission for its conversion" (p. 72).

10. For a recent, and comprehensive, analysis of the fall of Rome, see chap. 1, "The End of the World: How Rome Fell—and Why," in Thomas Cahill, *How the Irish Saved Civilization: The Untold Story of Ireland's Heroic Role from the Fall of Rome to the Rise of Medieval Europe* (New York: Doubleday, 1995).

11. Tomás Ó Fiaich, "Irish Monks on the Continent," in James P. Mackey, *An Introduction to Celtic Christianity* (Edinburgh: T&T Clark, 1989), p. 106.

12. Ibid., p. 104.

13. Bede's account of the Synod of Whitby is featured primarily in bk. 3, chap. 25, of his *Ecclesiastical History*, though he discussed the issues focused in the synod in many places.

14. This history is discussed in Nigel Pennick, *The Sacred World of the Celts* (New York: HarperCollins, 1997), pp. 94–95.

15. David J. Bosch, *Transforming Mission: Paradigm Shifts in Theology of Mission* (Maryknoll, N.Y.: Orbis Books, 1991), p. 294.

16. Ibid., p. 95. Bosch was referring to Catholic practice in the wake of the Enlightenment, but the principle predated the Enlightenment by more than one thousand years.

17. Nora Chadwick, *The Celts*, rev. ed. (London: Penguin Books, 1997), p. 222.

18. Bede, "The Lives of the Abbots of Wearmouth and Jarrow," in *The Age of Bede*, trans. D. H. Farmer (London: Penguin Books, 1988), pp. 185–208.

19. Ibid., p. 186.

20. Ibid., p. 189.

21. Ibid., p. 190.

22. See Bede's *Ecclesiastical History*, bk. 4, chap. 1.

23. In an endnote that purports to "explain" this sentence, the editors of the Oxford edition of Bede's *Ecclesiastical History* offer the unlikely explanation that, by "the custom of the Greeks" Bede refers to some kind of heterodox theological opinion, such as the Monothelete, or "one-energy" doctrine (Judith McClure and Roger Collins, eds.; Oxford and New York: Oxford University Press, 1994). This explanation is an unwarranted stretch, however, because Bede's allusions to heresies are usually quite explicit, and because the explanation is undermined by Bede's own explanation in his very next sentence: "Hadrian . . . waited four months for [Theodore's] hair to grow, that it might be shorn into the shape of a crown; for [Theodore] had [received] before the tonsure of St. Paul, the

apostle, after the manner of the eastern people." Bede reveals, in those two sequential sentences, that he virtually equated Roman customs with "the true faith," or at least that the true faith is totally dependent upon Roman forms for its protection and communication.

24. See Lyle E. Schaller, "European or American?" in chap. 7 of *The Interventionist* (Nashville: Abingdon Press, 1997), pp. 91–104. Schaller shows that all but one of the denominations "imported from Europe" are declining, and all but one of the denominations "made in America" are growing! The two exceptions actually prove Schaller's point. The Southern Baptist Convention, the one denomination imported from Europe that is growing, has reinvented itself several times. The Christian Church (Disciples of Christ), the one denomination "made in America" that is declining, represents the wing of the Restoration movement that marched to a European drum.

25. Schaller, in *The Interventionist*, demonstrates another two dozen comparisons between culturally European ways of doing church and culturally American ways of doing church. Anyone who has studied churches in two or more European countries has observed that the old European ways of doing church are not demonstratively more effective in Europe today than in the Unites States today.

26. Gustav Niebuhr, "Christianity's Rapid Growth Giving Africans New Voice," *Lexington Herald Leader*, December 13, 1998.

4. The Celtic Christian Community in Formation and Mission

1. *Recovering the Past: Celtic and Roman Mission* (London: Darton, Longman & Todd, 1996), p. 67.

2. Attributed to an Egyptian abbot named Moses, quoted in Esther de Waal, *The Celtic Way of Prayer: The Recovery of the Religious Imagination* (London: Hodder & Stoughton, 1996), p. 87.

3. See de Waal, *The Celtic Way of Prayer*, pp. 117–22 for a fuller description of the Celtic "soul friend" tradition. See John O'Donohue, *Anam Cara: A Book of Celtic Wisdom* (New York: Cliff Street Books, 1997), for powerful reflection from within the Irish soul friend tradition.

4. Small groups were prescribed in Rule 21 of the Benedictine Rule, as follows:

> If the community is rather large, some brothers chosen for their good repute and holy life should be made deans. They will take care of their groups of ten, managing all affairs according to the commandments of God and the order of their abbot. The deans selected should be the kind of men with whom the abbot can confidently share the burdens of his office.

5. De Waal, *The Celtic Way of Prayer*.

6. Ibid., p. 38.

7. Ibid., p. 43.

8. This translation is published in Oliver Davies and Fiona Bowie, *Celtic Christian Spirituality: An Anthology of Medieval and Modern Sources* (London: SPCK, 1995), pp. 41–43.

9. Much of the following approach is delineated in "The Rule of St. Benedict." For a recent English translation of Benedict's Rule, and an excellent commentary, see Esther de Waal, *A Life-Giving Way: A Commentary on the Rule of St. Benedict* (London: Geoffrey Chapman, 1995). Father Michael Rodgers, coauthor with Marcus Losack of *Glendalough: A Celtic Pilgrimage* (Harrisburg, Pa.: Morehouse Publishing, 1996), informs me that the Celtic monastic communities so substantially influenced the Benedictine monasteries on the Continent that, in the ministry of hospitality, the published Benedictine Rule reflects the ministry pattern of the Celtic communities.

10. Rule 66 of the Benedictine Rule provides that "at the door of the monastery, place a sensible old man who knows how to take a message and deliver a reply, and whose age keeps him from roaming about. The porter will need a room near the entrance so that visitors will always find him there to answer them."

11. John Finney, *Recovering the Past: Celtic and Roman Mission* (London: Darton, Longman & Todd, 1996).

12. John Finney, *Finding Faith Today: How Does It Happen?* (Swindon, U.K.: British and Foreign Bible Society, 1992).

13. Ibid., pp. 46–47.

5. How Celtic Christianity Communicated the Gospel

1. George A. Kennedy's translation of Aristotle, *On Rhetoric*, 2nd ed. (New York: Oxford University Press, 2007), is now the most useful English translation, although Lane Cooper's translation—Aristotle, *The Rhetoric of Aristotle* (Paramus, N.J.: Prentice-Hall, 1960)—is still the most widely cited. Edward P. J. Corbett and Robert J. Connors, *Classical Rhetoric for the Modern Student*, 4th ed. (New York: Oxford University Press, 1999), is an outstanding secondary source for discovering the strategic wisdom of Aristotle and the whole rhetorical tradition within Western scholarship.

2. Kennedy, *On Rhetoric*, p. 36.

3. Quoted in Lester Thonssen, A. Craig Baird, and Waldo W. Braden, *Speech Criticism*, 2nd ed. (New York: Ronald Press Company, 1970), p. 445.

4. From "Bishop Tirechan's Account of St. Patrick's Journey," in Liam de Paor, *Saint Patrick's World: The Christian Culture of Ireland's Apostolic Age* (Notre Dame, Ind.: University of Notre Dame Press, 1993), p. 171.

5. "Muirchu's Life of St. Patrick," in ibid., pp. 180–81.

6. See "Saint Patrick's Declaration" in ibid., p. 102.

7. Kennedy, *On Rhetoric*, p. 38.

8. Wayne N. Thompson, *The Process of Persuasion: Principles and Readings* (New York: Harper & Row, 1975), p. 59. Chap. 3 of Thompson's classic text gives a cogent review of the mid-1970s state of the art in ethos research and includes excerpts from a number of primary sources.

9. Helmut Thielicke, *The Trouble with the Church: A Call for Renewal*, ed. John W. Doberstein (New York: Harper & Row, 1965), pp. 1–11.

10. Kenneth Burke, *A Rhetoric of Motives* (Berkeley: University of California Press, 1969).

11. Søren Kierkegaard, *The Point of View*, trans. Walter Lowrie (London: Oxford University Press, 1939), p. 38. Kierkegaard also includes material on his "indirection" method in *Concluding Unscientific Postscript*, trans. David F. Swenson and Walter Lowrie (Princeton, N.J.: Princeton University Press, 1944), and Kierkegaard's *Attack upon "Christendom,"* trans. Walter Lowrie (Princeton, N.J.: Princeton University Press, 1946), and *Stages on Life's Way*, trans. Walter Lowrie (Princeton, N.J.: Princeton University Press, 1945). See also Raymond E. Anderson's classic article "Kierkegaard's Theory of Communication," *Speech Monographs* 30 (March 1963).

12. William Warren Sweet, *Revivalism in America* (Nashville: Abingdon Press, 1944), p. xii.

13. Walter Fisher, *Human Communication as Narration* (Columbia, South Carolina: University of South Carolina Press, 1987).

14. Maurice Charland, "Constitutive Rhetoric: The Case of the *Peuple Quebecois*," *The Quarterly Journal of Speech* 73, no. 2 (May 1987): 133–50.

15. John C. Hammerback and Richard J. Jensen, *The Rhetorical Career of Cesar Chavez* (College Station, Tex.: Texas A & M University Press, 1998).

16. Ibid., p. 55.

17. Thomas Cahill, *How the Irish Saved Civilization: The Untold Story of Ireland's Heroic Role from the Fall of Rome to the Rise of Medieval Europe* (New York: Doubleday, 1995), p. 109.

18. See de Paor, *Saint Patrick's World*, pp. 109–13.

19. Cahill, *How the Irish Saved Civilization*, p. 113. A few writers have not believed that Patrick identified with the Irish. R. C. P. Hanson, for instance, asserts that Patrick "had no particular love for the Irish. . . . He knew the Irish language. He knew something of the Irish society, . . . but he had no sympathy with Irish culture as such." See Hanson's article "The Mission of Saint Patrick," in James P. Mackey, *An Introduction to Celtic Christianity* (Edinburgh: T&T Clark, 1989), pp. 36–37. Hanson

bases that conclusion on his interpretation of several statements by Patrick that can be interpreted in other ways, and Hanson's interpretation is not usually the most obvious. Hanson, plausibly, argues that Patrick "certainly had no respect whatever for the religion of the Irish" (p. 37), a statement that warrants four responses. First, no one becomes a missionary to a people whose religion he or she greatly admires! Second, many missionaries, in every age, have identified with the receptor population without championing their religion! Third, as we will see in chap. 6, Patrick found things in their religion that Christianity could build on. Fourth, if the Irish people had not experienced Patrick identifying with them, they would not have responded to his message as they did.

20. See de Paor, *Saint Patrick's World*, pp. 175–97.

21. "Muirchu's Life of St. Patrick," in ibid., pp. 180–81.

22. Ibid, p. 187.

23. Ibid., pp. 184–85.

24. Adomnan of Iona, *Life of St. Columba*, trans. Richard Sharpe (London: Penguin Books, 1995).

25. Ibid., p. 105.

26. Ibid., pp. 179–80.

27. Bede, *The Ecclesiastical History of the English Nation*, trans. by L. C. Jane (New York: E. P. Dutton, 1910), bk. 3, chap 3.

28. Ibid., bk. 3, chap. 4.

29. Ibid., bk. 3, chaps. 5, 17.

30. Ibid., bk. 3, chap. 17.

31. Ibid., bk. 4, chap. 27.

32. Ibid., bk. 4, chap. 23.

33. Quoted in Thonssen, Baird, and Braden, *Speech Criticism*, p. 420.

34. Quoted in Cahill, *How the Irish Saved Civilization*, p. 6.

35. Cahill, *How the Irish Saved Civilization*, pp. 96–97.

36. Ibid., p. 126.

37. Ibid., p. 115.

38. George Campbell, *The Philosophy of Rhetoric* (Carbondale: Southern Illinois University Press, 1988).

39. This chart is adapted from Johnston McMaster, *The Future Returns: A Journey with Columba and Augustine of Canterbury* (Belfast: Corrymeela Press, 1997), p. 41.

40. Ian Bradley, *The Celtic Way* (London: Darton, Longman & Todd, 1993), p. 84.

41. Quoted in John T. McNeill, *The Celtic Churches: A History A.D. 200 to 1200* (Chicago and London: University of Chicago Press, 1974), p. 40.

42. Bradley, *The Celtic Way*, p. 85.

43. Ibid., p. 96.

44. Ibid., p. 90.

45. Ibid., pp. 1–2.

46. Ibid., p. 86.

47. Cahill, *How the Irish Saved Civilization*, p. 115.

6. The Missionary Perspective of Celtic Christianity

1. Adomnan admits that Columba preached to the Picts through an interpreter. See his ancient *Life of St. Columba* (New York: Penguin Books, 1995), p. 179.

2. David J. Bosch, *Transforming Mission: Paradigm Shifts in Theology of Mission* (Maryknoll, N.Y.: Orbis Books, 1991), p. 447.

3. Bede, *The Ecclesiastical History of the English Nation*, bk. 3, chap. 4.

4. Nora Chadwick, *The Celts*, rev. ed. (New York: Penguin Books, 1997), p. 197.

5. Twice, in the letter, Patrick refers to the Picts as "apostate." See "St. Patrick's Letter against the Soldiers of Coroticus," in Liam de Paor, *Saint Patrick's World* (Notre Dame, Ind.: University of Notre Dame Press, 1993), pp. 109, 112.

6. Ibid., p. 112.

7. Louis Gougaud, *Christianity in Celtic Lands: A History of the Churches of the Celts, Their Origin, Their Development, Influence, and Mutual Relations* (London: Sheed & Ward, 1932; repr., Dublin: Four Courts Press, 1992), pp. 26–27.

8. Quoted in W. Douglas Simpson, *Saint Ninian and the Origins of the Christian Church in Scotland* (Edinburgh: Oliver & Boyd, 1940), p. 91.

9. Bosch, *Transforming Mission*, p. 294.

10. Brendan Lehane, *The Quest of Three Abbots: The Golden Age of Celtic Christianity* (New York: Viking, 1968), p. 39.

11. Ibid., pp. 40, 111.

12. From "Bishop Tirechan's Account of St. Patrick's Journey," in de Paor, *Saint Patrick's World*, pp. 163–64.

13. From Douglas Hyde's *Carmina Gadelica*. Quoted in Oliver Davies and Fiona Bowie, *Celtic Christian Spirituality: An Anthology of Medieval and Modern Sources* (London: SPCK, 1995), p. 140.

14. Thomas Cahill, *How the Irish Saved Civilization: The Untold Story of Ireland's Heroic Role from the Fall of Rome to the Rise of Medieval Europe* (New York: Doubleday, 1995), p. 138.

15. Ibid., p. 126.

16. This summarizes material in chap. 5 of Cahill's *How the Irish Saved Civilization*, but no summary can do justice to Cahill's moving development of this theme.

17. Bede, *Ecclesiastical History*, bk. 2, chap. 9.

18. Ibid., bk. 2, chap. 9.

19. Ibid., bk. 2, chap. 14.

20. David Adam, *Flame in My Heart: St. Aidan for Today* (London: SPCK, 1997), pp. 96–98.

21. In the twentieth century, for instance, the experience of mission in the two-thirds world has enabled many Christian leaders to recover a Christian perspective on the supernatural and evil forces and Christ's role as Christus Victor, which were features of original Christianity but forgotten in the period of the Enlightenment's greatest influence on Western church thought.

22. From "Muirchu's Life of St. Patrick" in de Paor, *Saint Patrick's World*, p. 192.

23. Michael Mitton, *Restoring the Woven Cord: Strands of Celtic Christianity for the Church Today* (London: Darton, Longman & Todd, 1995), p. 58.

24. Indeed, one source suggests, "The Romans showed little love for the natural world and appear to have viewed it, like Plato before them, as a prison in which the soul is trapped." Roger Ellis and Chris Seaton, *New Celts* (Eastbourne: Kingsway Publications, 1998), p. 45.

25. Ian Bradley, *The Celtic Way* (London: Darton, Longman & Todd, 1993), pp. 53–54. All of chap. 3 is devoted to the theme "The Goodness of Nature."

26. Philip Sheldrake, in *Living between Worlds: Place and Journey in Celtic Spirituality* (Boston: Cowley Publications, 1996), p. 76, writes that, for Columbanus, "The 'incarnation,' as it were, of God in nature is . . . significant in two ways. First, it indicates unequivocally the closeness of God to us. . . . Secondly, nature is like a second revelation, a 'book' to be 'read' alongside the scriptures as we seek to deepen our knowledge of who God is."

27. Bradley, *The Celtic Way*, p. 52.

28. Ibid., pp. 59–60.

29. I have avoided discussion in the text of the Pelagian controversy. Pelagius was a British Celtic theologian whose name is given to the view of human nature that has prevailed, more or less, in British Christianity. Augustine once organized a council of bishops in Africa to declare Pelagius a heretic. Multiple motives may have driven this trial. Pelagius was a layman. He recognized, and mobilized, the minds of women. He

was obese, and some people, like Jerome, intensely disliked him. Most of his key writings, to which Augustine was reacting, have not survived. Pelagius appears to have affirmed free will and rejected predestination, and he may have believed in the possibility of universal salvation.

Although Pelagius's teachings undoubtedly influenced the Briton Celtic church, there are reasons to doubt any appreciable influence on the Irish, Pict, and Anglo-Saxon churches. One can detect no influence from Pelagius in Patrick's writings. Furthermore, the Irish monks who copied manuscripts did not know his writings or they did not prioritize their perpetuation. Nevertheless, Pelagius's theology was not a strong factor in Celtic Christianity's theological vision. Their instincts were probably semi-Pelagian, but they may have had no systematic theology of human nature, at least until Columbanus.

30. There is widespread interest today in the ancient religion of the Druids, although we don't know much about it. The fact that the Druids would not express their religious lore in writing, relying entirely on a twenty-year process of teaching it orally to the next generation of Druidic leaders, severely limits our knowledge of what they believed. Of course, that has not stopped some writers from pontificating, but most of these writers appear to be seeing their own reflection in the Druid pool of water!

31. "Bishop Tirechan's Account of St. Patrick's Journey," in de Paor, *Saint Patrick's World*, p. 169.

32. Mitton, *Restoring the Woven Cord*, pp. 90–91.

33. Ibid., p. 88.

34. "St. Patrick's Declaration," in de Paor, *Saint Patrick's World*, p. 98.

35. Derek Bryce, *Symbolism of the Celtic Cross* (York Beach, Maine: Samuel Weiser, 1995), p. 11.

36. Bede, *Ecclesiastical History*, bk. 1, chap. 30.

37. Ibid.

7. The Relevance of First-Millennium Celtic Christianity for Third-Millennium Western Christianity

1. I devoted chap. 6 of *Radical Outreach: The Recovery of Apostolic Ministry and Evangelism* (Nashville: Abingdon Press, 2003) to a case study of First Baptist Church, Leesburg.

2. Garrison Keillor, *Homegrown Democrat: A Few Plain Thoughts from the Heart of America*, rev. updated ed. (New York: Penguin, 2006), p. 46.

3. Often, much more American nationalism is attached to the folk understanding of Christianity than one could ever read from Scripture.

4. C. S. Lewis, *Mere Christianity* (New York: Macmillan, 1952), p. 199.

8. The Celtic Future of the Christian Movement in the West

1. For much more on the secular people theme, see George G. Hunter III, *How to Reach Secular People* (Nashville: Abingdon Press, 1992).

2. For a fuller explanation of the Enlightenment, modernity, and postmodernity, see George G. Hunter III, *Church for the Unchurched* (Nashville: Abingdon Press, 1996), chap. 1.

3. Indeed, many themes we rightly attach to Celtic Christianity—like imagination, love of nature, hospitality, or conversation with seekers—are not unique to the Celtic Christian movement.

4. Peter L. Berger and Thomas Luckmann, *The Social Construction of Reality: A Treatise in the Sociology of Knowledge* (New York: Doubleday, 1966).

5. Anne Wilson Schaef and Diane Fassel, *The Addictive Organization* (San Francisco: Harper & Row, 1988), p. 57.

6. Dick Schaefer, *Choices and Consequences: What to Do When a Teenager Uses Alcohol/Drugs* (Medina, Minn.: Johnson Institute, 1996), p. 34.

7. William L. White, *Pathways from the Culture of Addiction to the Culture of Recovery: A Travel Guide for Addiction Professionals*, 2nd ed. (Center City, Minn.: Hazelden, 1996).

8. Ibid., p. 56.

9. Ibid., p. 59.

10. Ibid., p. 54.

11. Ibid., pp. 268–75.

12. Ibid., pp. 395–407.

13. Ibid., pp. 375–85.

14. Ian Bradley, *The Celtic Way* (London: Darton, Longman & Todd, 1993), chap. 6.

15. George MacLeod interpreted his early vision for the modern Iona Community in *We Shall Rebuild: The Work of the Iona Community on Mainland and on Island* (Glasgow: Iona Community Publishing Department, 1994). That book focuses on the nature of, and need for, conversion and the mission of the congregation in helping people experience it, as well as the ways the Church must count in "the marketplace" through political and economic involvement. MacLeod's more mature reflections, on similar themes, are found in *Only One Way Left* (Glasgow: Iona Community, 1956).

16. Roger Ellis and Chris Seaton, *New Celts* (Eastbourne: Kingsway Publications, 1998), p. 76.

17. Ibid., p. 158.

18. The substance of the fifteen "talks" is featured in Nicky Gumbel, *Questions of Life* (Eastbourne: Kingsway Publications, 1995). Another

book by Nicky Gumbel, *Searching Issues* (Eastbourne: Kingsway Publications, 1995), which is for small-group leaders, addresses the seven questions that seekers ask most often in Alpha's small groups. Americans who are interested in the Alpha course can dial 1-800-36-ALPHA for these and other books, the interpretive video, and other Alpha resources.

19. "Why I Love Alpha, by the ex-prisoner whose favorite young people are the ones 'society says are no good,'" *Alpha News* (U.S. ed.), August-November, 1998, p. 8.

20. I describe these churches in Hunter, *Church for the Unchurched*. The book describes apostolic congregations, and chap. 4 describes the role of small groups in the life of these churches.

21. C. Peter Wagner, *Church Planting for a Greater Harvest* (Ventura, Calif.: Regal Books, 1990), p. 60.

22. Ibid., p. 62.

23. Charles L. Chaney, *Church Planting at the End of the Twentieth Century* (Wheaton, Ill.: Tyndale House, 1982), pp. 67–73.

24. I am indebted to my anthropologist colleague, Dr. Darrell Whiteman, for this poem.

25. Richard J. Mouw, *Consulting the Faithful: What Christian Intellectuals Can Learn from Popular Religion* (Grand Rapids: Eerdmans, 1994), p. 52.

26. Ibid., p. 55.

27. Simpson's version is found in Ray Simpson, *Exploring Celtic Spirituality* (London: Hodder & Stoughton, 1995), p. 170. Tristram's version was given in a presentation within the seminar "Celtic Models for Local Churches" at Holy Island, Lindisfarne, October 1998.

SELECTED BIBLIOGRAPHY
on Celtic Christianity

Adomnan of Iona. *Life of St. Columba*. Trans. Richard Sharpe. London: Penguin Books, 1995.

Arblaster, Paul D. J. *Celtic Christianity Yesterday, Today and for the Future: Gleaning Wisdom from the Primitive Protestants*. College Station, Tex.: Virtualbookworm.com Publishing, 2002.

Balzer, Tracy. *Thin Places: An Evangelical Journey into Celtic Spirituality*. Abilene, Tex.: Leafwood Publishers, 2007.

Bede. The Ecclesiastical History of the English Nation. Trans. L. C. Jane. New York: E. P. Dutton, 1910.

———. *The Ecclesiastical History of the English People*. Ed. Judith McClure and Roger Collins. Oxford and New York: Oxford University Press, 1994.

———. "Life of Cuthbert." In *The Age of Bede*, pp. 41–102. Rev. ed. London: Penguin Books, 1988.

———. "The Lives of the Abbots of Wearmouth and Jarrow." In *The Age of Bede*, pp. 185–208. Rev. ed. London: Penguin Books, 1988.

Bradley, Ian. *The Celtic Way*. London: Darton, Longman & Todd, 1993.

———. *Columba: Pilgrim and Penitent*. Glasgow: Wild Goose Publications, 1996.

———. *Celtic Christianity: Making Myths and Chasing Dreams*. New York: St. Martin's Press, 1999.

———. *Celtic Christian Communities*. Kelowna, British Columbia, Canada: Northstone Publishing Company, 2001.

Bryce, Derek. *Symbolism of the Celtic Cross*. York Beach, Maine: Samuel Weiser, 1995.

Bulloch, James. *The Life of the Celtic Church*. Edinburgh: Saint Andrew Press, 1963.

Cahill, Thomas. *How the Irish Saved Civilization: The Untold Story of Ireland's Heroic Role from the Fall of Rome to the Rise of Medieval Europe*. New York: Doubleday, 1995.

Carmichael, Alexander. *Carmina Gadelica: Hymns and Incantations*. Edinburgh: Floris Books, 1992.

Chadwick, Henry. *The Early Church*. Rev. ed. London: Penguin Books, 1993.

Chadwick, Nora. *The Celts*. Rev. ed. London: Penguin Books, 1997.

———. *The Age of the Saints in the Early Celtic Church*. Cardiganshire, Wales: Llanerch Publishers, 1960.

Clancy, Thomas Owen, and Gilbert Markus. *Iona: The Earliest Poetry of a Celtic Monastery*. Edinburgh: Edinburgh University Press, 1995.

Dales, Douglas. *Light to the Isles: Missionary Theology in Celtic and Anglo-Saxon Britain*. Cambridge: Lutterworth Press, 1997.

Davies, Oliver, ed. and trans. *Celtic Spirituality*. Mahwah, N.J.: Paulist Press, 1999.

Davies, Oliver, and Fiona Bowie. *Celtic Christian Spirituality: An Anthology of Medieval and Modern Sources*. London: SPCK, 1995.

De Paor, Liam. *Saint Patrick's World: The Christian Culture of Ireland's Apostolic Age*. Notre Dame, Ind.: University of Notre Dame Press, 1993.

De Waal, Esther. *The Celtic Way of Prayer: The Recovery of the Religious Imagination*. London: Hodder & Stoughton, 1996.

———. *Celtic Light: A Tradition Rediscovered*. London: HarperCollins, 1997.

———. *A Life-Giving Way: A Commentary on the Rule of St. Benedict*. London: Geoffrey Chapman, 1995.

Duncan, Anthony. *The Elements of Celtic Christianity*. Rockport, Mass.: Element Books, 1992.

Earle, Mary C., and Sylvia Maddox. *Holy Companions: Spiritual Practices from the Celtic Saints*. Harrisburg, Pa.: Morehouse Publishing, 2004.

Edwards, David L. *Christian England: Its Story to the Reformation*. Grand Rapids, Mich.: Eerdmans, 1980.

Ellis, Roger, and Chris Seaton. *New Celts*. Eastbourne: Kingsway Publications, 1998.

Fiaich, Tomás Ó. "Irish Monks on the Continent." In *An Introduction to Celtic Christianity* by James P. Mackey, pp. 101–39. Edinburgh: T&T Clark, 1989.

Finney, John. *Recovering the Past: Celtic and Roman Mission*. London: Darton, Longman & Todd, 1996.

Gougaud, Louis. *Christianity in Celtic Lands: A History of the Churches of the Celts, Their Origin, Their Development, Influence, and Mutual Relations*. London: Sheed & Ward, 1932. Reprint, Dublin: Four Courts Press, 1992.

Hanson, R. P. C. *Saint Patrick: His Origins and Career*. New York: Oxford University Press, 1968.

———. "The Mission of Saint Patrick." In *An Introduction to Celtic Christianity* by James P. Mackey, pp. 22–44. Edinburgh: T&T Clark, 1989.

Herren, Michael W., and Shirley Ann Brown. *Christ in Celtic Christianity: Britain and Ireland from the Fifth to the Tenth Century.* Suffolk, U.K.: Boydell Press, 2002.

Joyce, Timothy J. *Celtic Christianity: A Sacred Tradition, a Vision of Hope.* Maryknoll, N.Y.: Orbis Books, 1998.

Lehane, Brendan. *The Quest of Three Abbots: The Golden Age of Celtic Christianity.* New York: Viking, 1968.

Mackey, James P. *An Introduction to Celtic Christianity.* Edinburgh: T&T Clark, 1989.

———. "Introduction: Is There a Celtic Christianity?" In *An Introduction to Celtic Christianity* by James P. Mackey, pp. 1–21. Edinburgh: T&T Clark, 1989.

MacLeod, George. *We Shall Rebuild: The Work of the Iona Community on Mainland and on Island.* Glasgow: Iona Community Publishing Department, 1944.

———. *Only One Way Left.* Glasgow: Iona Community, 1956.

McMaster, Johnston. *The Future Returns: A Journey with Columba and Augustine of Canterbury.* Belfast: Corrymeela Press, 1997.

McNeill, John T. *The Celtic Churches: A History* A.D. *200 to 1200.* Chicago and London: University of Chicago Press, 1974.

Mayr-Harting, Henry. *The Coming of Christianity to Anglo-Saxon England.* London: B. T. Batsford, 1972.

Meek, Donald E. *The Quest for Celtic Christianity.* Edinburgh: Handsel Press, 2000.

Mitton, Michael. *Restoring the Woven Cord: Strands of Celtic Christianity for the Church Today.* London: Darton, Longman & Todd, 1995.

Murray, Patrick. *The Deer's Cry: A Treasury of Irish Verse.* Black Rock, County Dublin: Four Courts Press, 1986.

Newell, J. Philip. *Christ of the Celts: The Healing of Creation.* San Francisco: Jossey-Bass, 2008.

Northumbria Community. *Celtic Daily Prayer.* New York: HarperOne, 2002.

O'Donoghue, Noel Dermot. *Aristocracy of Soul: Patrick of Ireland.* London: Darton, Longman & Todd, 1987.

O'Donohue, John. *Anam Cara: A Book of Celtic Wisdom.* New York: Cliff Street Books, 1997.

Pennick, Nigel. *The Sacred World of the Celts.* London: HarperCollins, 1997.

Phillips, Andy. *An Forth Keltek: A Spiritual Pilgrimage with the Celtic Saints of Cornwall, Wales, and Brittany*. Truro, Cornwall, U.K: Spyrys a Gernow, 2009.

Rodgers, Michael, and Marcus Losack. *Glendalough: A Celtic Pilgrimage*. Harrisburg, Pa.: Morehouse Publishing, 1996.

Sellner, Edward C. *Wisdom of the Celtic Saints*. Notre Dame, Ind.: Ave Maria Press, 1993.

Sheldrake, Philip. *Living between Worlds: Place and Journey in Celtic Spirituality*. Boston: Cowley Publications, 1996.

Simpson, Ray. *Exploring Celtic Spirituality: Historic Roots for Our Future*. London: Hodder & Stoughton, 1995.

———, ed. *Celtic Blessings for Everyday Life: Prayers for Every Occasion*. London: Hodder & Stoughton, 1998.

Simpson, W. Douglas. *Saint Ninian and the Origins of the Christian Church in Scotland*. Edinburgh: Oliver & Boyd, 1940.

Taylor, Thomas. *The Life of St. Samson of Dol*. London: SPCK, 1925.

Thompson, E. A. *Who Was Saint Patrick?* Rochester, N.Y.: Boydell Press, 1985.

INDEX

Made in the USA
Lexington, KY
02 August 2018